THE AUSTRALIAN
Women's Weekly
Christmas
Bounty Books
DAY

Contents

Merry Christmas!

It's that time again when everyone starts getting a little bit edgy about the food they're going to serve over the Christmas holiday period. The key to success is to be organised ahead of time.

First establish how many people you have to feed and if they have any special dietary requirements. Decide if the meal is to be served indoors or outdoors. Consider your guest's ages and appetites and if the meal is to be formal, casual, or somewhere in between. With this information, work out a suitable menu. Think about your supply of tables, chairs, plates, cutlery, glasses, napery, serving bowls and platters.

Do you have enough oven and stove top space to suit the menu, and what about storage, fridge and freezer space?

Do you have the right sized pots, pans, bowls to accommodate larger quantities of food? Borrow, buy or hire things you're short of, do this ahead of time as everything will be in short supply the closer it gets to Christmas.

Order food ahead, especially ham, poultry and seafood, make shopping lists based on a countdown to the meal, from the pre-ordering down to shopping the day before.

Prepare and freeze whatever food you can, and prepare and refrigerate whatever you can as the day draws closer. Chop and prep whatever you can the day before the meal – and give yourself time to enjoy Christmas too!

DRINKS & STARTERS

PECORINO AND NIGELLA SEED BISCUITS

PREP + COOK TIME 1 HOUR (+ REFRIGERATION) **MAKES** 70

1½ cups (225g) plain (all-purpose) flour

1 teaspoon nigella seeds (see Tips)

150g (4½ ounces) butter, chopped coarsely

1¼ cups (100g) coarsely grated pecorino romano cheese

1 egg yolk

1 Sift flour into a large bowl, add seeds; rub in butter and cheese. Add egg yolk; mix to a firm dough. Wrap in plastic wrap; refrigerate for 1 hour.
2 Divide dough into two portions, roll each portion on a floured surface to 5mm (¼-inch) thick. Cut out stars using a 5cm (2-inch) star cutter; place shapes on greased oven trays. Refrigerate for 30 minutes.
3 Preheat oven to 180°C/350°F.
4 Bake biscuits for about 20 minutes; cool on trays.

TIPS
Nigella seeds are also called kalonji or black onion seeds; black on the outside and creamy-coloured on the inside, they have a sharp nutty flavour. They are available in most Asian and Middle Eastern food shops. Store biscuits in an airtight container for up to 1 week.
This biscuit dough can be shaped into a log, then wrapped tightly in plastic wrap and frozen. When you're ready, take it out of the freezer and leave it in the fridge to defrost. Slice the dough into 1cm (½-inch) rounds and place on a greased oven tray; bake the biscuits as directed above.

GREEN HUMMUS

PREP + COOK TIME 1¼ HOURS (+ SOAKING) MAKES 3 CUPS

You need to start this recipe the day before.

1 cup (200g) dried chickpeas (garbanzo beans)

1 clove garlic, crushed

¼ cup (70g) tahini

¼ cup (60ml) lemon juice

¼ cup (60ml) olive oil

½ cup firmly packed fresh coriander (cilantro) leaves

½ cup firmly packed fresh mint leaves

⅓ cup (65g) crumbled fetta

small coriander (cilantro) and mint leaves, extra

1 Place chickpeas in a medium bowl; cover with cold water. Stand overnight; drain.

2 Place drained chickpeas in a large saucepan with plenty of water. Bring to a simmer over high heat; simmer, uncovered, for 1 hour or until tender. Drain, reserving ½ cup cooking water.

3 Process chickpeas and reserved cooking water until smooth. Add garlic, tahini, juice, oil and herbs; process until smooth. Season to taste. Serve topped with fetta, extra coriander and mint leaves; drizzle with a little extra oil. Serve with pitta bread.

TIP Use 800g (1½ pounds) canned chickpeas instead of dried; drain, reserving ½ cup liquid. Use only if needed to thin hummus.

SCALLOPS WITH GINGER AND LEMON GRASS

PREP + COOK TIME 25 MINUTES
SERVES 8

24 scallops on the shell

10cm (4-inch) stalk fresh lemon grass (20g), white part only, chopped finely

2cm (¾-inch) piece fresh ginger (10g), grated finely

½ fresh long red chilli, seeded, chopped finely

2 teaspoons sesame oil

2 tablespoons mirin

1 tablespoon fish sauce

2 tablespoons lime juice

1 tablespoon finely chopped fresh coriander (cilantro)

1 Remove scallops from the shells. Rinse and dry shells; return scallops to shells.
2 Combine lemon grass, ginger, chilli, oil, mirin, sauce and juice in a small bowl. Spoon half the mixture over the scallops.
3 Cook scallops, on a heated grill plate (or grill or barbecue) over medium heat for 2 minutes or until just cooked through.
4 Spoon remaining lemon grass mixture over scallops. Serve sprinkled with coriander.

> **TIP** You could cook the scallops under a preheated grill (broiler) for about 2 minutes or until just cooked through.

POLENTA, BLUE CHEESE AND FIG TARTS

PREP + COOK TIME 20 MINUTES
MAKES 24

2 cups (500ml) milk

½ cup (80g) instant polenta (see Tips)

½ cup (40g) finely grated parmesan

2 tablespoons finely chopped fresh chives

24 x 6cm (2½-inch) small tart cases (220g)

12 small fresh figs (600g), halved lengthways

150g (5 ounces) blue cheese, crumbled

½ cup loosely packed fresh chervil sprigs

¼ cup (60ml) balsamic glaze

1   To make polenta, place milk in a small, heavy-based saucepan over medium heat; bring to a simmer. Whisking continuously, gradually add polenta in a thin stream; whisk for 5 minutes or until cooked and thickened (see Tips). Remove from heat; stir in parmesan and chives. Season to taste.

2   Place about 1 tablespoon of polenta into each tart shell. (If the polenta has thickened too much on standing, thin it by gradually whisking in a little extra milk.) Top with fig halves; sprinkle over blue cheese.

3   Place tarts on a large platter; top with chervil sprigs, drizzle with balsamic glaze.

TIPS Instant polenta, available from supermarkets, comes with cooking times varying from 1-5 minutes, so it's always best to read the packet directions. To keep polenta warm when serving, place polenta in a heatproof bowl placed over a saucepan of simmering water. Stir occasionally to prevent a skin from forming.
If fresh figs are out of season, substitute with dried figs.

MIDDLE-EASTERN SALAD CUPS

PREP + COOK TIME 40 MINUTES (+ COOLING) **MAKES** 28

You need 3 x 12-hole (2-tablespoon/40ml) deep flat-based patty pans; it's fine if you only have one pan, just make the cups in batches. You also need an 8cm (3¼-inch) round cutter.

1 large potato (300g), unpeeled

2 x 26cm (10½-inch) round pitta breads

¼ cup (60ml) olive oil

2 medium lebanese cucumbers (340g)

2 large tomatoes (440g), seeded, chopped finely

½ small red onion (50g), chopped finely

2 small red radishes (70g), trimmed, sliced thinly

extra sumac and small fresh flat-leaf parsley sprigs, to serve

SUMAC DRESSING

1 clove garlic, crushed

1 teaspoon sumac

1 teaspoon sea salt flakes

¼ cup (60ml) lemon juice

¼ cup (60ml) olive oil

1   Preheat oven to 200°C/400°F. Oil 3 x 12-hole (2-tablespoon/40ml) deep flat-based patty pans.

2   Boil, steam or microwave potato until just tender. When cool enough to handle, peel, chop finely; cool.

3   Meanwhile, place a piece of bread on a work surface. Using the 8cm round cutter, cut out seven bread rounds; separate rounds into two layers. Repeat with remaining bread; you will have 28 bread rounds. Brush inside (rough side) of each round with a little of the oil.

4   Firmly push bread rounds, oiled-side up, into pan holes. Bake for 5 minutes or until golden; cool.

5   Meanwhile, make sumac dressing.

6   Seed and finely chop one cucumber. Combine potato, chopped cucumber, tomato and onion in a medium bowl. Add dressing, stir gently to combine.

7   To serve, using a vegetable peeler, cut remaining cucumber into thin slices; place into each bread cup with a few slices of radish. Spoon 1 tablespoon of salad mixture into each bread cup; sprinkle with extra sumac, top with a parsley sprig, and fresh mint leaves, if you like.

SUMAC DRESSING   Combine ingredients in a small screw-top jar; shake well to combine.

> **TIP** Buy fresh, thin-style pitta bread; if the bread is too thick it may not sit well in the patty pan. Bread cups can be made a day ahead; store in an airtight container.

4 *Ways with* DRINKS

APPLE PIMM'S

PREP TIME 15 MINUTES **SERVES** 8

Combine 2 cups cucumber juice, 1⅓ cups Pimm's No 1, 1.5 litres (6 cups) chilled sparkling apple juice, 1 cup ginger wine, 1 thinly sliced lebanese cucumber, 1 thinly sliced red apple and 1 cup loosely packed fresh mint leaves in a large jug. Serve over ice.

> **TIPS** Juice about 800g (1½ pounds) peeled cucumbers in a juice separator. Or, puree peeled cucumber in a blender or processor. Strain into a jug and discard the solids. Pimm's No 1 is a gin-based alcohol flavoured with herbs.

MULLED 'WINE' MOCKTAIL

PREP + COOK TIME 20 MINUTES (+ REFRIGERATION) **SERVES** 8

Combine 2 litres (8 cups) red grape juice, 4 strips orange rind, 2 tablespoons light brown sugar, 2 cinnamon sticks, 12 cloves, 3 fresh bay leaves and 2 sprigs fresh thyme in a large saucepan. Simmer, uncovered, for 10 minutes (do not boil). Cool; refrigerate until cold. Strain mixture into a large jug; discard solids. Add 1 thinly sliced small orange, extra fresh bay leaves and fresh sprigs of thyme to mixture. Serve over ice.

LYCHEE AND LIME MUDDLE

PREP + COOK TIME 30 MINUTES (+ REFRIGERATION)
SERVES 8

Thinly slice 12 fresh kaffir lime leaves and a 6cm (2¼-inch) piece fresh ginger; place in a small saucepan with 2 cups water and ¼ cup grated dark palm sugar. Stir over medium heat until sugar dissolves; bring to the boil. Reduce heat; simmer, uncovered, until reduced to 1½ cups. Strain syrup into a medium heatproof jug; discard solids. Cool; refrigerate until cold. Divide 1kg (2lbs) seeded lychees, 1 quartered and thinly sliced lime, 1⅓ cups white rum, ⅓ cup lime juice and the syrup into eight glasses; gently crush and mix with a muddling stick (or the handle of a thick wooden spoon or a pestle). Top with ice and 2 cups chilled soda water.

TIP A muddling stick is a bartender's tool used to crush or mash fruits, herbs and spices in the bottom of a glass to release their flavour.

SPARKLING RASPBERRY

PREP TIME 25 MINUTES (+ REFRIGERATION) **SERVES** 8

Combine 180g (6oz) fresh or frozen raspberries, ⅓ cup strawberry-flavoured liqueur, ⅓ cup orange-flavoured liqueur, 1 tablespoon caster (superfine) sugar and the zested rind of ½ small orange in a small bowl. Refrigerate 20 minutes, stirring occasionally, until sugar dissolves. Divide mixture into eight glasses; top with 3 cups (750ml) chilled sparkling white wine.

TIP Use a zesting tool to make the long thin strips of rind.

DUKKAH-CRUSTED LAMB WITH SMOKED EGGPLANT DIP

PREP + COOK TIME 40 MINUTES (+ REFRIGERATION & STANDING) **MAKES** 12

1 tablespoon olive oil

2 tablespoons dukkah (see Tips)

600g (1¼ pounds) lamb backstraps

extra olive oil and small fresh flat-leaf parsley sprigs, to serve

EGGPLANT DIP

1 large eggplant (500g)

1 clove garlic, crushed

1 teaspoon sea salt flakes

1 teaspoon ground cumin

1 tablespoon finely chopped fresh flat-leaf parsley

2 tablespoons tahini

¼ cup (60ml) lemon juice

1 Combine oil, dukkah and lamb in a medium bowl; cover, refrigerate 2 hours.
2 Meanwhile, make eggplant dip.
3 Stand lamb at room temperature for 15 minutes. Heat an oiled grill plate or frying pan over medium heat. Cook lamb for 3 minutes each side (for medium rare) or until cooked as desired. Cover lamb; rest for 5 minutes before slicing thinly, season.
4 In small serving bowls or plates, top 1 tablespoon of dip with 3 slices of lamb; drizzle with extra oil and top with a parsley sprig.

EGGPLANT DIP

Prick eggplant all over with a fork. Grill over medium heat on an oiled grill plate for 25 minutes, turning frequently, or until tender. When cool enough to handle, peel eggplant. Squeeze eggplant flesh to remove any excess juice. Blend or process eggplant with remaining ingredients until smooth. Season to taste.

TIPS You will need 12 small serving bowls or plates and decorative bamboo forks or skewers to serve.
You can barbecue the lamb, instead of grilling or pan-frying, if you like.
Dukkah is a packaged spice and nut blend; it is available from spice shops, major supermarkets and delis.
The eggplant dip can be made a day ahead; store, covered, in the fridge. The lamb can be marinated a day ahead; store, covered, in the fridge.

SUMAC BEEF CARPACCIO WITH BASIL OIL

PREP + COOK TIME 30 MINUTES (+ FREEZING) **SERVES** 6

500g (1-pound) trimmed beef fillet

1½ teaspoons ground sumac

2 teaspoons finely chopped thyme

½ cup (40g) shaved pecorino (see Tips)

¼ cup (25g) chopped walnuts, toasted

⅓ cup fresh micro red veined sorrel

BASIL OIL

¼ cup firmly packed fresh basil leaves

½ cup (125ml) olive oil

1 tablespoon white balsamic vinegar

1 Place beef onto a board; season well with cracked pepper, sea salt, sumac and thyme, rubbing evenly all over. Using your hands, press beef into a thick log; roll up tightly in plastic wrap, twisting ends to tighten. Tie a knot in each end. Freeze for 6 hours.

2 Meanwhile, make basil oil.

3 Peel back half the plastic wrap from beef; using a sharp knife, slice beef as thinly as possible, peeling back remaining plastic wrap as you go. Arrange beef, in a single layer, on a large serving platter; season. Drizzle with basil oil; sprinkle with pecorino, walnuts and sorrel. Serve immediately.

BASIL OIL

Place basil in a small heatproof bowl, pour boiling water over the leaves; stand for 5 seconds. Drain. Refresh basil in another bowl of iced water; drain well. Pat basil dry with paper towel. Heat oil in a small saucepan over low heat for 2 minutes. Remove pan from heat; stir in basil. Blend or process oil mixture with vinegar until smooth; season to taste. Cover surface with plastic wrap.

SERVING SUGGESTION Serve with fresh crusty bread.

TIPS Use the best quality beef you can for carpaccio and always keep it well chilled. To save time, ask the butcher to trim the beef for you. Pecorino is a hard Italian sheep's milk cheese similar to parmesan which may be used instead, if you like.

GRAVLAX

PREP TIME 30 MINUTES (+ REFRIGERATION) **SERVES** 12

*You will need to start this recipe
2 days ahead.*

½ cup (150g) rock salt

½ cup (110g) white (granulated) sugar

⅔ cup coarsely chopped fresh dill

2 teaspoons finely grated lime rind

2 teaspoons white peppercorns, crushed

1 tablespoon dried juniper
berries, crushed (see Tips)

⅓ cup (80ml) gin

750g (1½-pound) centre-cut piece salmon
fillet, skin-on, bones removed

2 tablespoons lime juice

2 tablespoons olive oil

crème fraîche and toasted slices of french
bread, to serve

HERB SALAD

2 punnets micro herbs, trimmed

¼ cup fresh dill sprigs

1   Combine salt, sugar, dill, rind, pepper, juniper berries and gin in a medium bowl. Spread half the gin mixture over the base of a shallow 20cm x 28cm (8-inch x 11¼-inch) glass or ceramic dish. Place salmon, skin-side down, over mixture. Top with remaining gin mixture.
2   Cover salmon with plastic wrap. Place another dish on top, weigh down with cans of food. Refrigerate for 24-36 hours, turning salmon every 12 hours.
3   Remove salmon from dish; scrape away any loose mixture, discard gin mixture. Pat salmon dry with paper towel. Holding a knife at a 45 degree angle, and using long strokes, slice salmon across the grain as thinly as possible. Arrange slices on a large platter.
4   Just before serving, make herb salad.
5   Drizzle salmon with juice and oil. Serve salmon and herb salad with toasted bread and crème fraîche.

HERB SALAD
Combine ingredients in a small bowl.

TIPS You can substitute vodka for gin or leave out the alcohol completely. Micro herbs are small punnets of various baby herbs or cress available at greengrocers or growers' markets. Alternatively, use the smallest torn leaves from a regular bunch of herbs.
Juniper berries are available from spice shops, delis and greengrocers.

CRUNCHY SALT AND PEPPER PRAWNS WITH SWEET CHILLI SYRUP

PREP + COOK TIME 45 MINUTES (+ STANDING) **MAKES** 30

30 uncooked medium prawns (shrimp) (1.3kg)

¾ cup (55g) panko (japanese) breadcrumbs

1 teaspoon cracked black peppercorns

1½ teaspoons piri piri seasoning

2 teaspoons sea salt flakes

1 egg white, beaten lightly

vegetable oil, for deep-frying

1 fresh long red chilli, sliced thinly

2 tablespoons fresh coriander (cilantro) leaves

SWEET CHILLI SYRUP

½ cup (110g) white (granulated) sugar

½ cup (125ml) water

¼ cup (80g) sweet chilli sauce

4 kaffir lime leaves, torn

1cm (½-inch) piece fresh ginger (5g), sliced thinly

2 fresh coriander (cilantro) roots and stems, washed, sliced thinly

1 Make sweet chilli syrup.

2 Shell and devein prawns leaving tails intact.

3 Combine crumbs, pepper, seasoning and salt in a small bowl. Holding prawns by the tail, dip one at a time into egg white, then coat in crumb mixture.

4 Fill a large saucepan or deep-fryer one-third full with oil; heat to 180°C/350°F (or until a cube of bread turns golden in 10 seconds). Deep-fry prawns, in batches, for 1 minute or until cooked through and crisp. Drain on paper towel.

5 Sprinkle prawns with chilli and coriander leaves; accompany with sweet chilli syrup for dipping.

SWEET CHILLI SYRUP

Combine ingredients in a small saucepan; stir over medium heat until sugar dissolves. Bring to the boil. Reduce heat; simmer, uncovered, about for 5 minutes or until sauce thickens slightly. Remove from heat; stand for 15 minutes, then discard lime leaves.

TIPS The sauce can be made up to 2 days ahead; store, covered, in the fridge. Prawns can be crumbed 3 hours ahead; store, covered, in the fridge.

HEIRLOOM TOMATO SALAD WITH PROSCIUTTO

PREP + COOK TIME 10 MINUTES **SERVES** 6

12 thin slices prosciutto (180g)

130g (4 ounces) buffalo mozzarella

500g (1 pound) heirloom tomatoes, sliced

250g (8 ounces) mixed baby or cherry tomatoes, halved

½ cup loosely packed fresh basil leaves

6 slices sourdough bread (420g)

CHILLI DRESSING

2 tablespoons olive oil

2 tablespoons red wine vinegar

1 clove garlic, crushed

¼ teaspoon chilli flakes

1 teaspoon caster (superfine) sugar

1 Make chilli dressing.
2 Tear prosciutto and mozzarella into pieces.
3 Place prosciutto and mozzarella in a large bowl with all the tomatoes, basil and dressing; toss gently to combine.
4 Cook bread on a heated oiled barbecue (or grill or grill plate) until toasted both sides.
5 Serve salad on a platter with grilled bread.

CHILLI DRESSING

Whisk ingredients in a small bowl until combined. Season to taste.

MAINS
& SIDES

TURKEY ROLL WITH CHERRY AND ALMOND STUFFING

PREP + COOK TIME 2 HOURS 30 MINUTES (+ STANDING) **SERVES** 10

3kg (6-pound) double turkey breasts, boned, skin on

20g (¾ ounce) butter, melted

1 tablespoon plain (all-purpose) flour

⅓ cup (80ml) tawny port

¾ cup (180ml) dry white wine

1 cup (250ml) chicken stock

2½ cups (375g) fresh cherries, seeded, quartered

CHERRY AND ALMOND STUFFING

30g (1 ounce) butter

7 shallots (175g), chopped finely

4 cloves garlic, chopped finely

½ cup coarsely chopped fresh marjoram

2 cups (330g) cooked brown rice

1 cup (150g) fresh cherries, seeded, quartered

¼ cup (35g) dried cherries (see Tips)

½ cup (80g) almond kernels, roasted, chopped coarsely

2 eggs

1   Preheat oven to 200°C/400°F.

2   Make cherry and almond stuffing.

3   To butterfly turkey, place breasts, skin-side down, on a chopping board; starting from centre of breasts, split one breast in half horizontally, stopping about 1cm (½ inch) from the end, open out flap. Repeat on the other side; you should now have one long piece. Use hands to flatten the turkey meat.

4   Place cherry and almond stuffing at one end of turkey; roll up tightly from short side. Use kitchen string to secure at 2.5cm (1-inch) intervals along roll. Brush with butter; season. Place turkey in a flameproof dish with enough water to barely cover the base of dish. Roast for 1½ hours or until cooked through. Add more water to dish as necessary during cooking to prevent juices burning. To test if turkey is cooked, insert a skewer into the thickest part of the roll; remove skewer and press the flesh. Juices should run clear. Cover roll with foil; stand for 20 minutes.

5   Meanwhile, pour pan juices into a medium jug; skim fat, then return 1 tablespoon of fat to baking dish. Place dish over medium heat; stir in flour, cook, stirring, until well browned. Add port; bring to the boil. Add wine, stock and reserved pan juices; stir until gravy boils and thickens. Add cherries; simmer, uncovered, for 2 minutes or until softened. Season to taste.

6   Serve sliced turkey with gravy.

CHERRY AND ALMOND STUFFING

Melt butter in a small frying pan; cook shallot and garlic until browned lightly. Combine with remaining ingredients in a large bowl; season.

> **TIPS** Order turkey breasts from your butcher and ask him to bone and butterfly them for you.
> Dried cherries are available from specialty food stores. If unavailable, use dried cranberries.
> To make shallots easier to peel, pour boiling water over shallots in a heatproof bowl; stand for 1 minute. Skins will slip off easily. You need to cook ⅔ cup brown rice for this recipe.

DOUBLE ORANGE-GLAZED HAM

PREP + COOK TIME 2 HOURS **SERVES** 20

8kg (16-pound) cooked leg of ham

2 cups (500ml) water

sprigs of fresh herbs (rosemary and bay leaves), to decorate

DOUBLE ORANGE GLAZE

300g (9½ ounces) orange
(or blood orange) marmalade

¼ cup (75g) firmly packed dark brown sugar

¼ cup (60ml) freshly squeezed orange (or blood orange) juice

1 Preheat oven to 180°C/350°F. Score through the ham rind about 10cm (4 inches) from the shank end of the leg.
2 To remove the rind, run your thumb around the edge of the rind just under the skin. Start pulling the rind from the widest edge of the ham; continue to pull the rind carefully away from the fat up to the score line. Remove the rind completely. (Reserved rind can be used to cover the cut surface of the ham to keep it moist during storage.)
3 Using a large sharp knife, score across the fat at 3cm (1¼-inch) intervals, cutting just through the surface of the top fat. Do not cut too deeply or the fat will spread apart during cooking.
4 Make double orange glaze.
5 Place the ham on a wire rack in a large roasting pan; pour 1½ cups of the water into the dish. Brush the ham well with the glaze. Cover the shank end with foil.
6 Bake ham for 1 hour 20 minutes or until browned all over, brushing occasionally with the glaze during cooking, and adding the remaining water if needed.
7 Decorate ham with fresh herbs, to serve.

DOUBLE ORANGE GLAZE
Stir ingredients in a small bowl until combined. Season to taste.

> TIPS For a smaller leg or half leg of ham, halve the glaze recipe. Rind will remove more easily from the ham if it's warmed in a slow (150°C/300°F) oven for 30 minutes. If the glaze becomes too thick to brush on, reheat until it reaches the correct consistency.
> The glaze is suitable to microwave in a microwave-safe glass or ceramic container; don't use plastic as the glaze will get very hot.

4 *Ways with* SIDE SALADS

PRESERVED LEMON AND MINT COUSCOUS

PREP + COOK TIME 15 MINUTES **SERVES** 4

Cook 250g (8oz) pearl couscous in a saucepan of boiling water until tender; drain. Place couscous in a large bowl with ½ cup currants, 1 teaspoon ground cumin, 2 tablespoons finely chopped preserved lemon rind, 1 cup fresh mint leaves and ¼ cup lemon juice; toss gently to combine. Season to taste.

ROASTED CORN SALAD

PREP + COOK TIME 30 MINUTES **SERVES** 6

Cook 4 trimmed corn cobs on a heated oiled grill plate (or grill or barbecue) until browned all over. When cool enough to handle, cut kernels from cobs. Place kernels in a medium bowl with 1 thinly sliced small red onion, 2 coarsely chopped large avocados, 250g (8oz) halved cherry tomatoes, 2 tablespoons lime juice and ¼ cup fresh micro coriander (cilantro) leaves; toss gently to combine. Season to taste.

GREEN APPLE SLAW

PREP TIME 15 MINUTES **SERVES** 4

Cut 2 large unpeeled green apples into matchsticks. Place in a large bowl with 1 cup finely shredded green cabbage, 1 thinly sliced green onion (scallion), ¼ cup small fresh mint leaves, 2 tablespoons extra virgin olive oil and 2 tablespoons lemon juice; toss gently to combine. Season to taste.

WILD RICE SALAD WITH SPINACH AND FIGS

PREP + COOK TIME 15 MINUTES **SERVES** 8

Cook 2 cups wild rice blend in a large saucepan of boiling water until tender; drain. Rinse under cold water; drain. Place in a large bowl. Place 2 teaspoons finely grated orange rind, ½ cup orange juice, 2 tablespoons olive oil and 1 tablespoon white balsamic vinegar in a screw-top jar; shake well. Add dressing to rice with ¾ cup coarsely chopped roasted pecans, ½ cup thinly sliced dried figs, 100g (3oz) baby spinach leaves and 2 thinly sliced green onions (scallions); toss gently to combine. Season to taste.

ROLLED LAMB SHOULDER WITH HARISSA AND COUSCOUS STUFFING

PREP + COOK TIME 1 HOUR 30 MINUTES **SERVES** 8

⅓ cup (65g) couscous

⅓ cup (80ml) boiling water

2 x 750g (3-pound) boned lamb shoulders

¼ cup (40g) pine nuts, roasted

½ cup coarsely chopped fresh mint

1 tablespoon olive oil

HARISSA

2 medium red capsicums
(bell peppers) (400g)

1 tablespoon olive oil

1 small red onion (100g),
chopped coarsely

4 cloves garlic, chopped coarsely

1 tablespoon ground coriander

1 tablespoon caraway seeds

2 teaspoons ground cumin

1 fresh red thai (serrano) chilli,
chopped coarsely

1 tablespoon finely chopped preserved
lemon rind

¼ cup fresh mint leaves

1 Preheat oven to 200°C/400°F.

2 Make harissa.

3 Combine couscous with the water in a medium bowl; stand for 5 minutes. Mix harissa into couscous.

4 Place lamb, fat-side down, on a chopping board. Spread couscous mixture over lamb; top with pine nuts and mint. Roll tightly to enclose filling; secure with kitchen string at 2cm (¾-inch) intervals.

5 Heat oil in a large baking dish over medium heat; add lamb, cook until browned all over. Transfer dish to oven; roast, uncovered, for 45 minutes. Cover lamb with foil; stand for 10 minutes before serving.

HARISSA

Place capsicums on an oven tray; roast in oven for 20 minutes or until skin blisters and blackens (leave the oven on). Cover capsicums with plastic wrap for 5 minutes; peel away skin, discard stems and seeds. Heat oil in a small frying pan; cook onion and garlic, stirring, until softened. Add spices; cook, stirring, until fragrant. Process capsicum and onion mixture with remaining ingredients until smooth.

SERVING SUGGESTION Serve with grilled flat bread and rocket; accompany with greek-style yoghurt.

WARM CHICKEN, LABNE AND MAPLE WALNUT SALAD

PREP + COOK TIME 1 HOUR SERVES 6

500g (1 pound) baby beetroot (beets)

¼ cup (60ml) olive oil

300g (9½ ounces) unpeeled pumpkin, cut into thin wedges

¾ cup (75g) walnuts

2 tablespoons pure maple syrup

600g (1¼ pounds) chicken breast fillets

1½ tablespoons sherry vinegar

2 teaspoons wholegrain mustard

1 teaspoon dijon mustard

125g (4 ounces) mixed salad leaves

100g (3 ounces) drained labne

1   Preheat oven to 200°C/400°F.
2   Trim beetroot, leaving 2.5cm (1 inch) of stems attached; halve beetroot. Place in a baking dish; drizzle with 1 tablespoon of the oil. Bake for 15 minutes.
3   Add pumpkin to beetroot, bake for a further 25 minutes or until vegetables are tender.
4   Meanwhile, place nuts on a baking-paper-lined oven tray; drizzle with syrup. Bake for 10 minutes or until browned, stirring halfway through. Cool.
5   Preheat barbecue (or grill or grill plate) on high heat. Brush chicken with 2 teaspoons of the oil; season. Cook chicken until browned on both sides and cooked through. Transfer to a plate. Cover; stand for 5 minutes.
6   Meanwhile, combine vinegar, mustards and remaining oil in a small bowl. Season to taste.
7   Slice chicken thickly. Arrange salad leaves on a serving platter; top with pumpkin, beetroot, chicken, nuts and labne. Drizzle with dressing.

TIP Labne is available from delicatessens and some supermarkets.

POACHED DUCK AND CASHEW SALAD WITH DUCK CRACKLING

PREP + COOK TIME 1 HOUR **SERVES** 6

3 duck breasts (450g)

2 cups (500ml) chicken stock

½ cup (125ml) salt-reduced
soy sauce

2 star anise

½ cup (125ml) vegetable oil

¼ cup (65g) grated palm sugar

½ cup (75g) roasted
unsalted cashews

150g (4½ ounces) dried rice
vermicelli noodles

2 lebanese cucumbers (260g)

1 large carrot (180g),
cut into matchsticks

2 purple shallots (50g), sliced thinly

1 fresh long red chilli, sliced thinly

1 cup (80g) bean sprouts

⅓ cup loosely packed
fresh mint leaves

⅓ cup loosely packed fresh
coriander (cilantro) leaves

⅓ cup loosely packed fresh thai
basil leaves

LIME DRESSING

1 clove garlic, crushed

1½ tablespoons grated
palm sugar

1½ tablespoons fish sauce

⅓ cup (80ml) lime juice

¼ cup (60ml) peanut oil

1 Remove skin from duck breasts. Place duck breast, stock, soy and star anise in a medium saucepan; bring to the boil. Reduce heat; simmer, uncovered, for 3 minutes. Remove from heat. Cool duck in poaching liquid.

2 Meanwhile, heat oil in a small frying pan; cook duck skin until crisp. Remove with a slotted spoon; drain on paper towel. Drain fat from pan.

3 Heat a cleaned frying pan over medium heat; cook sugar and nuts, stirring, for 5 minutes or until caramelised. Pour onto a baking-paper-lined oven tray; cool.

4 Make lime dressing.

5 Place noodles in a large heatproof bowl, cover with boiling water; stand until just tender. Drain; return noodles to bowl.

6 Halve cucumber lengthways; remove seeds. Cut cucumber into matchsticks. Add cucumber to noodles with carrot, shallots, chilli, sprouts and ½ cup of the dressing; toss gently to combine.

7 Thinly slice duck and duck skin. Coarsely chop nuts.

8 Add herbs to salad; toss gently to combine.

9 Serve salad topped with duck; sprinkle with skin and nuts, drizzle with remaining dressing.

LIME DRESSING
Stir ingredients in a small bowl until sugar dissolves.

4 *Ways with* POLENTA AND MASH

LUXE POTATO MASH

PREP + COOK TIME 30 MINUTES **SERVES** 4

Place 1kg (2lbs) potatoes in a medium saucepan with enough cold water to barely cover them. Boil, uncovered, over medium heat, for 15 minutes or until potato is tender; drain. Wipe pan dry. Mash potatoes in a heatproof bowl, or use a potato ricer, until smooth. Melt 60g (2oz) butter with ¾ cup mascarpone in same pan over medium heat; stir in mash and 30g (1oz) blue cheese. Season with salt and pepper. Serve topped with another 30g (1oz) crumbled blue cheese.

> **TIP** Floury and all-rounder potatoes are best for mash; try coliban, toolangi delight, king edward or dutch cream.

CRISP POLENTA

PREP + COOK TIME 30 MINUTES (+ REFRIGERATION) **SERVES** 4

Grease a deep 20cm (8-inch) square cake pan; line base and sides with baking paper. Make Soft Polenta (see recipe, opposite), using instant polenta and 3 cups stock; cook for 10 minutes. Pour mixture into pan. Cover; refrigerate for 3 hours or until firm. Preheat oven to 220°C/425°F. Line a large oven tray with baking paper. Remove polenta from pan; cut into 20 chips. Place chips on tray; sprinkle with ¾ cup grated parmesan, turn to coat all sides. Bake for 15 minutes or until golden and crisp. Season with flaked salt.

> **TIP** Polenta can also be barbecued or grilled. Brush with a little olive oil and barbecue or char-grill until browned and a crust forms. Turn once and brown the other side.

SOFT POLENTA

PREP + COOK TIME 30 MINUTES **SERVES** 4

Bring 1 litre (4 cups) stock, water or milk (or half stock and half milk) to the boil in a large deep saucepan. Add 1 cup (170g) polenta in a thin steady stream and whisk until the mixture comes to the boil. Reduce heat to low; cook, stirring, with a long-handled wooden spoon or whisk, for about 25 minutes until soft and thick. Stir in 30g (1 ounce) chopped butter and ½ cup (40g) grated parmesan. Season to taste. Adjust the consistency with a little extra milk if needed. Serve immediately.

OLIVE OIL AND SAGE MASH

PREP + COOK TIME 35 MINUTES **SERVES** 4

Place 1kg (2lbs) potatoes in a medium saucepan with enough cold water to barely cover them. Boil, uncovered, over medium heat, for 15 minutes or until potato is tender; drain. Wipe pan dry. Heat ⅓ cup olive oil in same pan; fry 2 thinly sliced cloves garlic and 2 tablespoons sage leaves until crisp. Remove with a slotted spoon. Return potatoes to pan with ½ cup hot milk; mash until smooth. Season with salt and ground black pepper. Serve topped with garlic and sage.

BARBECUED FILLET OF BEEF WITH CARAMELISED ONION AND RADISH

PREP + COOK TIME 1 HOUR 10 MINUTES (+ REFRIGERATION & STANDING) **SERVES** 6

You will need to start this recipe the day before.

1.5kg (3-pound) piece beef eye fillet

1 cup (250ml) dry red wine

4 cloves garlic, sliced thinly

½ teaspoon cracked black peppercorns

4 fresh bay leaves

4 fresh thyme sprigs

1 tablespoon olive oil

60g (2 ounces) trimmed watercress

CARAMELISED ONION AND RADISH

¼ cup (55g) caster (superfine) sugar

¼ cup (60ml) white wine vinegar

1 medium red onion (170g), cut into thin wedges

6 radishes (240g), cut into wedges

4 cloves garlic, sliced thinly

1 Trim fillet of any fat and membrane. Tuck thin end of fillet underneath. Using kitchen string, tie beef firmly at 2cm (¾-inch) intervals to keep its shape. Combine wine, garlic, pepper, bay leaves and thyme in dish; add beef, turn to coat in marinade. Cover, refrigerate overnight, turning three times.

2 Remove beef from marinade; discard marinade. Pat beef dry with paper towel; brush with oil, season.

3 Cook beef on a heated barbecue until browned all over. Cover with lid or foil; cook for 45 minutes for medium or until done as desired. Transfer beef to a heated plate; cover with foil, stand 20 minutes.

4 Meanwhile, make caramelised onion and radish.

5 Serve sliced beef with caramelised onion and radish, topped with watercress.

CARAMELISED ONION AND RADISH

Heat a medium frying pan, add sugar; cook over medium heat until sugar turns golden brown. Carefully add vinegar, as sugar will bubble fiercely; stir until sugar dissolves. Bring to the boil; simmer, uncovered, until syrupy. Stir in onion, radishes and garlic; simmer for 5 minutes or until onion softens.

BARBECUED CHILLI AND TAMARIND BEEF WITH VEGETABLES

PREP + COOK TIME 1 HOUR (+ REFRIGERATION & STANDING) **SERVES** 6

1kg (2 pounds) beef rump steak

2 medium carrots (240g), cut into matchsticks

3 lebanese cucumbers (390g), cut into matchsticks

½ cup (125ml) white wine vinegar

1 tablespoon white (granulated) sugar

1 teaspoon salt

½ cup loosely packed small fresh coriander (cilantro) leaves

¼ cup finely shredded fresh mint

1¼ cups (100g) bean sprouts

½ cup (70g) roasted unsalted peanuts, chopped coarsely

¼ cup loosely packed small fresh mint leaves, extra

CHILLI AND TAMARIND MARINADE

6 dried long red chillies

3 dried small red thai (serrano) chillies

1 fresh long red chilli

4 purple shallots (100g), chopped

6 cloves garlic, crushed

1 tablespoon finely chopped coriander (cilantro) roots

½ cup (125ml) tamarind concentrate

¼ cup (60ml) fish sauce

¼ cup (55g) white (granulated) sugar

1 Make chilli and tamarind marinade.

2 Place beef in a shallow dish. Add marinade; turn beef to coat in marinade. Cover; refrigerate 6 hours or overnight, turning occasionally.

3 Drain beef from marinade; reserve marinade. Cook beef on a heated oiled grill plate (or grill or barbecue) over high heat, for 10 minutes, turning once, or until cooked as desired. Transfer to a plate; cover, stand for 20 minutes.

4 Meanwhile, bring reserved marinade to the boil in a small saucepan; simmer, uncovered, for 5 minutes. Cool.

5 Combine carrot and cucumber in a medium bowl.

6 Heat vinegar, sugar and salt in a small saucepan over low heat; stir, without boiling, until sugar is dissolved. Bring to the boil. Pour over vegetables; cool. Add coriander, mint and sprouts.

7 Thinly slice beef, drizzle with reserved marinade. Serve beef topped with vegetables, nuts and extra mint.

CHILLI AND TAMARIND MARINADE

Dry-fry dried chillies in a medium frying pan, stirring, until blackened. Cool. Using a mortar and pestle, grind to a fine powder. Add fresh ingredients, one at a time; grind to a paste. Stir in tamarind, sauce and sugar.

TIPS Adjust the amount of chilli in the marinade to suit your taste as it is very hot. Tamarind concentrate is available from Asian and Indian grocery stores or in the Asian section of most major supermarkets.

TOMATO AND GOAT'S CHEESE TART WITH RICE AND SEED CRUST

PREP + COOK TIME 1 HOUR (+ COOLING) **SERVES** 8

500g (1 pound) packaged ready-steamed brown basmati rice

⅓ cup (50g) sesame seeds

1½ cups (120g) finely grated parmesan

3 eggs

1 teaspoon sea salt flakes

500g (1 pound) fresh ricotta (see Tips)

150g (4½ ounces) soft goat's cheese

¼ cup (60ml) milk

1 tablespoon wholegrain mustard

1 clove garlic, chopped finely

400g (12½ ounces) mixed heirloom tomatoes, halved and sliced (see Tips)

2 tablespoons small fresh basil leaves

1 tablespoon extra virgin olive oil

2 teaspoons balsamic vinegar

1 Preheat oven to 200°C/400°F. Grease a deep 24cm (9½-inch) round springform pan.

2 Process rice, seeds and half the parmesan until rice is finely chopped. Add 1 egg and half the salt; process until mixture forms a coarse dough.

3 Using damp hands, press rice dough over base and up the side of the pan, stopping 5mm (¼ inch) from the top.

4 Bake crust for 25 minutes or until golden and dry to the touch.

5 Meanwhile, process ricotta, goat's cheese, milk, mustard and garlic with remaining parmesan, eggs and salt until smooth.

6 Pour cheese mixture into warm rice crust. Reduce oven to 180°C/350°F; bake tart for a further 30 minutes or until a skewer inserted into the centre comes out clean. Cool for 1 hour.

7 Just before serving, arrange tomatoes and basil on top of tart; drizzle with oil and vinegar. Season with freshly ground black pepper.

TIPS Ready-steamed brown basmati rice is available in packets from the rice section of supermarkets.
Use fresh ricotta, sold in wheels from delis and the deli section of supermarkets for the best taste and texture.
If heirloom tomatoes are not available, use baby grape or cherry truss tomatoes instead.

BARBECUED PRAWNS WITH CHILLI LIME DRESSING

PREP + COOK TIME 35 MINUTES
SERVES 8

1.7kg (3½ pounds) uncooked large king prawns (shrimp)

2 baby fennel bulbs (260g), sliced thinly

250g (8 ounces) baby cucumbers, sliced thinly lengthways

6 watermelon radishes (210g), sliced thinly

¼ cup fresh baby coriander (cilantro)

CHILLI LIME DRESSING

⅓ cup (80ml) lime juice

⅓ cup (80ml) lemon juice

½ cup (125ml) olive oil

2 cloves garlic, crushed

2 teaspoons caster (superfine) sugar

2 teaspoons sea salt flakes

1 fresh long green chilli, sliced thinly

1   Make chilli lime dressing.
2   Carefully cut through back of prawns, without cutting all the way through, leaving heads and shells intact; devein prawns. Combine prawns in a large bowl with half the dressing; cook prawns on a heated oiled grill plate (or grill or barbecue), until just changed colour.
3   Place fennel, cucumber and radishes in a medium bowl; toss gently to combine.
4   Serve prawns on salad, drizzled with remaining dressing and topped with coriander.

CHILLI LIME DRESSING
Combine ingredients in a small bowl.

> **TIP** Watermelon radishes are available from specialist greengrocers. If you can't find them, use the regular red variety.

LOBSTER WITH FENNEL SALAD

PREP TIME 35 MINUTES
(+ STANDING) **SERVES** 6

1 medium fennel bulb (300g)

150g (5 ounces) curly endive

3 cooked lobsters (1.8kg),
halved lengthways

GREEN OLIVE AND
CURRANT SALSA
3 medium lemons (420g)

⅓ cup (70g) seeded small green olives,
chopped coarsely

2 tablespoons drained baby capers, rinsed

2 tablespoons dried currants

⅓ cup finely chopped fresh
flat-leaf parsley

2 tablespoons olive oil

1 Make green olive and currant salsa.
2 Reserve fronds from fennel. Slice fennel thinly with a V-slicer or mandoline. Combine fennel and endive in a medium bowl, sprinkle with half the salsa.
3 Divide lobsters and salad among plates. Drizzle with remaining salsa; sprinkle with reserved fronds.

GREEN OLIVE AND CURRANT SALSA
Finely grate rind from one lemon. Peel rind thickly from all lemons to remove white pith. Segment lemons over a medium bowl to catch juice. Chop lemon flesh finely; add to bowl with grated rind and remaining ingredients. Stand for 20 minutes. Season to taste.

> **TIP** Christmas is one of those special occasions in the year when you can spoil your family with the luxury of lobster. Purchased cooked lobster (from your fishmonger) coupled with a simple dressed salad of fennel and endive, makes this dish very easy and quick to make.

BARBECUED SQUID AND CHORIZO WITH BLACK OLIVE DRESSING

PREP + COOK TIME 1 HOUR (+ REFRIGERATION) **SERVES** 6

1kg (2 pounds) cleaned small squid hoods

1 teaspoon smoked paprika

2 cloves garlic, crushed

2 medium red capsicums
(bell peppers) (400g)

2 medium yellow capsicums
(bell peppers) (400g)

2 uncooked chorizo sausages (250g),
sliced thickly

6 thick slices bread (270g)

½ cup (125ml) olive oil

BLACK OLIVE DRESSING
½ cup (80g) seeded black olives,
chopped coarsely

½ cup coarsely chopped fresh
flat-leaf parsley

⅓ cup (80ml) olive oil

¼ cup (60ml) sherry vinegar

1 clove garlic, crushed

¼ teaspoon smoked paprika

1 Cut squid in half lengthways, then cut diagonally crossways into 3cm (1¼-inch) strips. Combine squid, paprika and garlic in a medium bowl. Cover; refrigerate 1 hour.
2 Cook capsicums on a heated grill plate (or grill or barbecue), until skin blisters and blackens. Cover capsicums with plastic or paper for about 5 minutes; peel away skin then slice thinly, place in a medium bowl. Discard seeds and membranes.
3 Cook chorizo on heated grill plate (or grill or barbecue) for 5 minutes or until chorizo is crisp. Cook squid for 2 minutes or until barely tender.
4 Meanwhile, make black olive dressing.
5 Combine squid, chorizo and capsicum on a platter; drizzle with dressing.
6 Brush both sides of bread with oil; toast both sides on heated grill plate (or grill or barbecue). Serve alongside salad.

BLACK OLIVE DRESSING
Combine ingredients in a medium bowl; season to taste.

SERVING SUGGESTION **Serve with a rocket (arugula) salad.**

BARBECUED OCEAN TROUT WITH SALSA CRIOLLA

PREP + COOK TIME 40 MINUTES **SERVES** 6

2 teaspoons sea salt flakes

1 tablespoon extra virgin olive oil

1.2kg (2½-pound) ocean trout fillet, skin on, pin-boned

2 tablespoons coarsely chopped fresh flat-leaf parsley

2 cloves garlic, crushed

1 medium lemon (140g), cut into wedges

SALSA CRIOLLA

350g (11 ounces) baby heirloom tomatoes, halved or quartered

1 large vine-ripened tomato (220g), cut into wedges

1 shallot (25g), sliced thinly

½ medium red onion (85g), sliced thinly

2 tablespoons extra virgin olive oil

1 tablespoon red wine vinegar

⅓ cup loosely packed fresh oregano

1 Make salsa criolla.

2 Preheat a covered barbecue with all burners on low and hood closed until temperature reaches 200°C/400°F, or follow manufacturer's instructions.

3 Combine salt and half the oil in a small bowl; rub mixture on skin side of fish. Combine parsley, garlic and remaining oil in a small bowl; rub mixture on flesh side of fish. Season.

4 Place fish on barbecue grill, skin-side down, with the hood down. Turn burners off underneath fish then turn other burners to high. Cook in covered barbecue for 15 minutes or until cooked as desired (ocean trout is best served medium-rare in the thickest part).

5 Transfer fish using two large fish or egg slices to a platter. Serve with salsa criolla and lemon wedges.

SALSA CRIOLLA

Combine ingredients, except oregano, in a medium bowl. Season to taste. Just before serving, add oregano; toss to combine.

TIPS Salsa criolla is a South American version of salsa, containing sliced onion with any combination of tomato, capsicum, boiled potatoes and coriander, and is served with seafood, meat or rice. Salmon or whole white fish could be used instead of the ocean trout. If you like, cut slits into the thickest part of the fish and rub the oil mixture into the cuts. You can also serve the salsa criolla with pan-fried or barbecued fish fillets

4 *Ways with* VEGETABLE SIDES

BRUSSELS SPROUTS, DUKKAH AND HONEY

PREP + COOK TIME 15 MINUTES **SERVES** 4

Trim ends from 500g (1lb) brussels sprouts; cut in half. Place in a bowl with 2 tablespoons each honey and olive oil. Season with salt and pepper; toss well to combine. Heat a large non-stick frying pan over medium heat; cook sprouts, cut-side down, for 2 minutes or until tender. Turn over; cook for 2 minutes or until tender. Add 2 tablespoons dukkah; toss to combine.

SILVER BEET WITH PINE NUTS

PREP + COOK TIME 20 MINUTES **SERVES** 4

Trim 6cm (2½-in) from stem ends of 380g (12oz) silver beet (swiss chard); discard. Chop remaining silver beet coarsely, keeping leaves and white stem separate. Heat ¼ cup olive oil in a frying pan over medium heat; cook 1 large thinly sliced red onion, white stems and ⅓ cup raisins, stirring, for 5 minutes. Add leaves; stir 8 minutes or until tender. Stir in ½ cup toasted pine nuts.

BROCCOLINI AND CRUMBS

PREP + COOK TIME 20 MINUTES **SERVES** 4

Heat ⅓ cup olive oil in a frying pan over medium heat; stir ¾ cup panko (japanese) breadcrumbs and 1 teaspoon salt flakes for 5 minutes or until golden. Add 4 cloves thinly sliced garlic; stir for 3 minutes or until cooked. Add ¼ cup fresh flat-leaf parsley and 1 teaspoon grated lemon rind. Boil 460g (14½oz) trimmed broccolini for 3 minutes until tender. Drain; toss with crumb mixture.

ZUCCHINI AND ALMONDS

PREP + COOK TIME 15 MINUTES **SERVES** 4

Cut 6 small zucchini lengthways into four. Heat ⅓ cup olive oil in a frying pan over medium heat; cook zucchini, in two batches, for 3 minutes each side or until golden. Remove with tongs or a slotted spoon. Add ½ cup flaked natural almonds to pan; cook, stirring, for 3 minutes or until golden. Return zucchini to pan; toss to combine. Season and serve with lemon cheeks.

WHOLE FISH WITH GINGER AND GREEN ONIONS

PREP + COOK TIME 35 MINUTES **SERVES** 4

Other fish to try whole are: barramundi, bream and river trout. Allow about 400g (12½ ounces) per person, and adjust the number of fish depending on their size.

2 x 800g (1½-pound) whole snapper, cleaned

¼ teaspoon ground white pepper

8cm (3¼-inch) piece fresh ginger, peeled, cut into long thin strips

3 green onions (scallions), trimmed, sliced thinly

2 tablespoons light soy sauce

2 tablespoons chinese cooking wine (shao hsing)

½ teaspoon caster (superfine) sugar

1 teaspoon sesame oil

1 fresh long red chilli, seeded, sliced thinly on the diagonal

2 tablespoons peanut oil

1 cup loosely packed fresh coriander (cilantro) leaves

1 Preheat oven to 200°C/400°F.

2 Pat fish dry with paper towel then make three deep cuts through the flesh on each side.

3 Take four large sheets of baking paper and rinse under cold water to make the paper pliable. Place two sheets in a cross pattern on each of two oven trays; place a fish in the centre of each. Sprinkle both sides of the fish with pepper; top with half the ginger and the white part of the green onion. Bring the sides of the paper together and seal by folding over, then wrap over the remaining sides, tucking the short sides under to form a sealed parcel.

4 Bake fish for 20 minutes. To test if the fish is cooked, check in one of the cuts; the flesh should be white. Insert a fork into the thickest part; the flesh should come away from the bone easily.

5 Meanwhile, stir soy sauce, cooking wine, sugar and sesame oil in a small bowl until sugar dissolves.

6 Transfer fish to a platter; top with chilli, drizzle with soy dressing.

7 Heat peanut oil in a small saucepan, add remaining ginger; cook, stirring for 2 minutes or until golden. Spoon oil and ginger over fish. Top with coriander.

SERVING SUGGESTION Serve with steamed rice and greens, such as buk choy, choy sum, broccolini or snow peas.

TIPS You can use 4 plate-sized fish and wrap each individually, if you prefer, so each diner gets their own parcel.
Check if the fish is ready after 12 minutes cooking time.

CHICKPEA, FARRO, ORANGE AND CHERRY SALAD

PREP + COOK TIME 45 MINUTES **SERVES** 4

1½ cups (300g) farro or barley (see Tips)

500g (1 pound) butternut pumpkin, cut into 1.5cm (¾-inch) pieces

1 tablespoon olive oil

2 teaspoons cumin seeds

2 medium oranges (480g)

400g (12½ ounces) canned chickpeas (garbanzo beans), drained, rinsed

⅓ cup (55g) almonds, roasted, chopped coarsely

¼ cup (35g) sunflower seeds, toasted lightly

300g (9½ ounces) cherries, halved, pitted

¼ cup coarsely chopped fresh mint

2 tablespoons torn fresh flat-leaf parsley

2 tablespoons pomegranate molasses

½ cup (125ml) extra virgin olive oil

2 tablespoons small fresh mint leaves, extra

1 Preheat oven to 220°C/425°F.

2 Cook farro in a large saucepan of boiling water for 35 minutes or until tender; drain. Rinse under cold water; drain well.

3 Meanwhile, combine pumpkin, olive oil and cumin seeds on a large oven tray; season. Bake for 20 minutes or until tender and beginning to brown around edges.

4 Remove rind from oranges with a zester, cut into long thin strips. Segment oranges over a bowl to catch the juices then squeeze the membrane; reserve 2 tablespoons of juice.

5 Place farro, pumpkin, orange segments and rind in a large bowl with chickpeas, almonds, sunflower seeds, cherries and herbs. Combine reserved orange juice, pomegranate molasses and extra virgin olive oil in a small jug. Drizzle dressing over salad, season to taste; toss to combine. Serve salad topped with extra mint.

> **TIPS** This textural salad of grains, nuts and fruit can be eaten as a light lunch or serve it as a side dish with chicken or lamb.
> Grapes would make a nice alternative to the cherries.
> Farro is a grain related to wheat with a similar delicious nutty taste, however unlike wheat and spelt, which can take hours to cook, it is relatively fast-cooking. You will find it in health food stores.

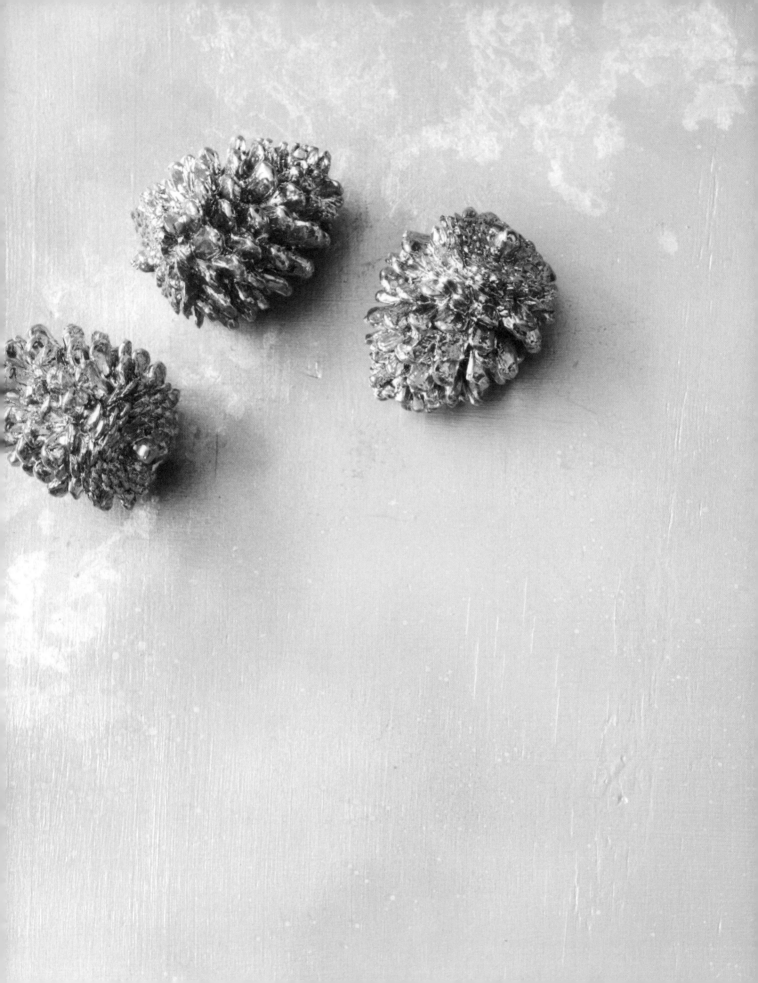

CAKES, PUDDINGS & DESSERTS

LEMON BERRY CAKE WITH YOGHURT CUSTARD

PREP + COOK TIME 2 HOURS **SERVES** 10

250g (8 ounces) butter

1 tablespoon finely grated lemon rind

1½ cups (330g) caster (superfine) sugar

3 eggs

1½ cups (225g) self-raising flour

½ cup (75g) plain (all-purpose) flour

½ cup (140g) greek-style yoghurt

⅓ cup (80ml) lemon juice

450g (14½ ounces) frozen mixed berries

YOGHURT CUSTARD

4 egg yolks

300ml pouring cream

½ cup (110g) caster (superfine) sugar

1 cup (280g) greek-style yoghurt

1 Preheat oven to 160°C/325°F. Grease a deep 22cm (9-inch) square cake pan; line base and sides with baking paper, extending the paper 5cm (2 inches) over sides.

2 Beat butter, rind and sugar in a small bowl with an electric mixer until light and fluffy. Beat in eggs, one at a time. Transfer to a large bowl; stir in sifted flours, yoghurt and juice, in two batches. Spread half the mixture into pan; sprinkle with half the frozen berries. Top with remaining cake batter, then remaining berries.

3 Bake cake about 1½ hours. Leave cake in pan for 10 minutes before turning, top-side up, onto a wire rack.

4 Meanwhile, make yoghurt custard.

5 Serve cake warm with yoghurt custard.

YOGHURT CUSTARD

Stir egg yolks, cream and sugar in a small saucepan, over low heat, without boiling, until mixture thickens. Remove from heat; stir in yoghurt.

TIP Make sure the butter and eggs are at room temperature before you start this recipe.

HONEY AND SAFFRON PEARS

PREP + COOK TIME 45 MINUTES (+ COOLING) **SERVES** 6

6 small firm pears (1kg)

¼ cup (60ml) lemon juice

¼ teaspoon saffron threads

1 cup (350g) honey

2 cups (500ml) water

¾ cup (165g) caster (superfine) sugar

¼ cup (60ml) water, extra

1 Peel pears; place in a large bowl, cover with cold water, stir in juice.

2 Dry-fry saffron in a medium saucepan (large enough to fit the upright pears), stirring, over low heat for 1 minute or until fragrant. Add honey and the water; bring to the boil. Reduce heat; simmer, uncovered, for 3 minutes. Add drained pears upright; simmer, covered until pears are just tender. Remove pears with a slotted spoon to a medium bowl; cool pears. Bring honey mixture to the boil; boil, uncovered, until liquid is reduced by half. Cool syrup.

3 Meanwhile, combine sugar and the extra water in a small saucepan; stir over high heat, without boiling, until sugar dissolves. Bring to the boil. Reduce heat; simmer, uncovered, without stirring, until caramel in colour. Remove from heat; allow bubbles to subside.

4 To make toffee nests; place a sheet of baking paper on the bench. Dip two forks into toffee; working over the paper, with forks back to back, quickly pull the forks back and forth against each other to make thin strands of toffee. Working quickly, gather up the strands and shape into a nest. Place nest on serving plate. Repeat with remaining toffee to make five more nests.

5 Sit a pear in the middle of each nest; drizzle with honey syrup. Serve immediately.

TIP The toffee nests can be made up to an hour before serving if the weather is cool.

4 *Ways with* FOOLS

RHUBARB AND GINGER BEER FOOLS

PREP + COOK TIME 15 MINUTES (+ COOLING) **SERVES** 4

Combine 500g (1 pound) coarsely chopped, trimmed rhubarb, with 2 teaspoons finely grated ginger, ¼ cup (60ml) ginger beer and 2 tablespoons caster (superfine) sugar in a medium saucepan over high heat. Bring to the boil. Reduce heat to medium; simmer, stirring occasionally, for 7 minutes or until rhubarb is tender. Transfer to a tray to cool. Meanwhile, beat 300ml thickened (heavy) cream in a small bowl with an electric mixer until firm peaks form. Spoon three-quarters of the rhubarb mixture onto cream; do not stir. Spoon cream mixture into four ⅔ cup (160ml) glasses. Top with remaining rhubarb and ¼ cup (55g) crushed gingernut biscuits.

> **TIP** Rhubarb mixture can be made a day ahead; store refrigerated in an airtight container.

CHERRY AND LEMONADE FOOLS

PREP + COOK TIME 15 MINUTES (+ COOLING) **SERVES** 4

Pit 225g (7 ounces) fresh cherries, reserving 4 cherries on the stem to serve. Place pitted cherries and ⅓ cup (80ml) lemonade in a small frying pan over high heat; bring to the boil. Reduce heat; simmer for 5 minutes, mashing with a fork a few times during cooking, or until cherries soften slightly and liquid thickens slightly. Cool. Meanwhile, beat 300ml thickened (heavy) cream in a small bowl with an electric mixer until soft peaks form. Fold ⅓ cup (110g) ready-made lemon curd and ⅓ cup (15g) toasted coconut flakes into cream. Spoon three-quarters of the cherry mixture onto cream mixture; do not stir. Spoon cream mixture into four ⅔ cup (160ml) glasses. Top with remaining cherry mixture, reserved cherries and 1 tablespoon extra toasted coconut.

PEACH AND VANILLA YOGHURT FOOLS

PREP + COOK TIME 10 MINUTES **SERVES** 4

Halve 4 medium peaches (600g), discard stones; quarter each half. Process half the peaches with 2 tablespoons caster (superfine) sugar and ¼ teaspoon vanilla extract until smooth. Place 2 cups (560g) vanilla yoghurt in a medium bowl. Spoon three-quarters of the peach puree onto yoghurt; do not stir. Spoon yoghurt mixture into four ⅔ cup (160ml) glasses. Top with remaining puree, remaining peaches, 2 tablespoons coarsely chopped pistachios and 1 tablespoon small mint leaves.

BLUEBERRY AND ORANGE FOOLS

PREP + COOK TIME 10 MINUTES (+ COOLING) **SERVES** 4

Combine 125g (4 ounces) blueberries, 1 tablespoon caster (superfine) sugar, 2 teaspoons finely grated orange rind and ¼ cup (60ml) orange juice in a small frying pan over high heat; bring to the boil. Reduce heat; simmer for 3 minutes, stirring occasionally or until blueberries soften slightly and liquid thickens slightly. Cool. Fold 2 teaspoons finely grated orange rind into 2 cups (550g) thick ready-made custard. Spoon three-quarters blueberry mixture over custard; do not stir. Spoon custard mixture into four ⅔ cup (160ml) glasses. Top with remaining blueberry mixture, 6 sponge finger biscuits (130g) and 60g (2 ounces) blueberries. Serve immediately.

TIP You will need 1 orange for this recipe.

KOUGLOF

PREP + COOK TIME 1¾ HOURS (+ STANDING) SERVES 20

200g (6½ ounces) unsalted butter

½ cup (75g) raisins

¼ cup (60ml) kirsch

2 teaspoons finely grated orange rind

16 almond kernels

3⅓ cups (500g) plain (all-purpose) flour

1 teaspoon coarse cooking salt

½ cup (110g) caster (superfine) sugar

5 teaspoons (14g) dried yeast

¾ cup (180ml) warm milk

4 eggs

½ cup (70g) slivered almonds

2 teaspoons icing (confectioners') sugar

1 Chop butter; stand at room temperature. Combine raisins, kirsch and rind in a small bowl.

2 Grease a 24cm (9½-inch) (top measurement) kouglof pan well. Place almond kernels in grooves of mould; refrigerate pan.

3 Sift flour and salt into a large bowl of an electric mixer with dough hook attached; add caster sugar, yeast, milk and eggs. Knead on low speed for about 1 minute or until mixture forms a soft dough. Add butter. Increase speed to about medium; knead for about 10 minutes or until dough is smooth and elastic. Add raisin mixture and slivered almonds; knead until combined. Cover bowl; stand in a warm place for about 1 hour or until dough has doubled in size.

4 Punch down dough; knead with electric mixer for 1 minute. Gently push dough into pan, to avoid disturbing the nuts. Cover; stand in warm place for about 1 hour or until dough has doubled in size.

5 Meanwhile, preheat oven to 180°C/350°F.

6 Bake kouglof about 40 minutes. Stand kouglof in pan for 5 minutes, before turning onto wire rack to cool. Serve dusted with sifted icing sugar.

TIPS You will need an electric mixer fitted with a dough hook for this recipe as the dough is too soft to knead by hand. This is a traditional cake from north-eastern France; you find similar cakes in Germany, Austria and eastern Europe (the names vary slightly: Kugelhopf, Gugelhupf). It is traditionally baked in a circular pan with a central tube made of enamelled pottery but you can easily find metal pans in kitchen stores.

SERVING IDEAS Serve warm with whipped cream. It keeps well and is delicious the following day thickly sliced, toasted and spread with butter and jam.

STORAGE Cake will keep in an airtight container at room temperature for about 1 week.

CHRISTMAS ETON MESS WREATH

PREP + COOK TIME 30 MINUTES (+ FREEZING) **SERVES** 6

250g (8 ounces) raspberries

1 tablespoon icing (confectioners') sugar, plus extra to dust

300g (9½ ounces) white chocolate melts

200g (6½ ounces) coconut macaroons, quartered

6 raspberry macarons

6 strawberry macarons

250g (8 ounces) small strawberries

200g (6½ ounces) cherries

1 medium pomegranate (320g), halved, broken into small pieces

25g (¾ ounce) mini plain meringues

edible flowers (optional), to serve

¾ cup (180ml) thickened (heavy) cream, whipped

1   Place 75g (2½ ounces) of the raspberries in an airtight container; freeze for 2 hours.

2   Process frozen raspberries until finely chopped; return to the container, freeze until required. In the same food processor bowl, process 125g (4 ounces) of the raspberries with icing sugar until pureed. Push puree through a fine sieve over a small bowl; cover, refrigerate until required.

3   Place two sheets of baking paper, slightly overlapping on a work surface to create a wider sheet. Using a 40cm (16-inch) bowl, trace a round. Using a second 30cm (12-inch) bowl, trace a second round in the centre of the first round. You will now have a template for the chocolate ring.

4   Stir chocolate in a heatproof bowl over a saucepan of gently simmering water (don't allow the bowl to touch the water) until melted. Using template as a guide, drop spoonfuls of chocolate in ring, then using the back of a spoon, spread chocolate thickly and evenly to fill ring. Stand until set.

5   Carefully lift chocolate ring off paper and transfer to a large serving board. Place coconut macarons and macaroons equally around the ring, layering with strawberries, cherries (you can halve a few cherries and remove the stones if you like), pomegranate and remaining raspberries. Crush mini meringues over the wreath, sprinkle with the chopped frozen raspberries and fresh flowers, if using. Dust with icing sugar and drizzle with a little raspberry sauce. Serve wreath with remaining raspberry sauce and whipped cream in separate small bowls, for guests to help themselves.

TIP Macarons, often sold or labelled as 'macaroons', are the French-style sandwiched biscuits, whilst macaroons are traditionally the single chewy coconut and egg white biscuits. We have used both in this recipe.

WATERMELON BAKLAVA TRIFLE

PREP TIME 30 MINUTES **SERVES** 8

The trifle is ready to eat immediately or is best eaten within 4 hours of assembling. You will need about half a seedless watermelon for this recipe.

500g (1 pound) firm full-milk ricotta

1 cup (280g) greek-style yoghurt

¼ cup (90g) honey

1 teaspoon orange blossom water

3 teaspoons zested or finely sliced lime rind

1 cup (240g) sour cream

2.5kg (5 pounds) seedless watermelon

600g (1¼ pounds) baklava

¼ cup (45g) coarsely chopped pistachios

1 Process ricotta, yoghurt, honey, orange blossom water and 2 teaspoons of the rind until smooth. Add sour cream; process in short bursts until thickened. (Take care not to over-process or the mixture will split).

2 Remove rind from watermelon; cut into 5mm (¼-inch) thick slices. Using a 5.5cm (2¼-inch) cutter, cut out rounds. Reserve 6 pieces for the top.

3 Cut baklava into approximate 2cm x 5cm (¾-inch x 2-inch) finger-shaped pieces (depending on the baklava, you may simply need to cut it in half.) Reserve 3 pieces for the top of the trifle.

4 Place half the baklava, cut side out, in a single layer in a 3-litre (12-cup) capacity tall glass serving vessel. Top with a third of the ricotta mixture, half the watermelon and a third of the pistachios; repeat layering, finishing with ricotta mixture, pistachios and reserved watermelon and baklava pieces. Sprinkle with remaining rind.

GLUTEN-FREE FRUIT AND ALMOND LOAVES

PREP + COOK TIME 2 HOURS 35 MINUTES (+ STANDING & COOLING) **MAKES** 2

*You need to begin this recipe
1 week ahead.*

1kg (2 pounds) mixed dried fruit

1 tablespoon finely grated orange rind

⅔ cup (160ml) sweet sherry

150g (4½ ounces) butter, softened

⅔ cup (150g) firmly packed dark brown sugar

4 eggs

100g (3 ounces) marzipan, chopped coarsely

1 small apple (130g), grated coarsely

¾ cup (100g) ground almonds

1¼ cups (185g) gluten-free plain (all-purpose) flour

1 cup (160g) blanched almonds

¼ cup (60ml) sweet sherry, extra

1 Combine fruit, rind and sherry in a large bowl; mix well. Cover with plastic wrap; stand in a cool, dark place for one week, stirring every day.

2 Preheat oven to 150°C/300°F. Line bases and sides of two 9cm x 21cm (3¼-inch x 8½-inch) loaf pans with two layers of baking paper, extending paper 5cm (2 inches) above sides.

3 Beat butter and sugar in small bowl with an electric mixer until just combined. Beat in eggs, one at a time. Mix butter mixture into fruit mixture. Stir in marzipan, apple, ground almonds and sifted flour. Spread mixture into pans; decorate with nuts.

4 Bake loaves for about 2 hours. Brush hot loaves with extra sherry, cover with foil; cool in pans.

MANGO PAN TART

PREP + COOK TIME 45 MINUTES
(+ REFRIGERATION & COOLING)
SERVES 6

125g (4 ounces) butter, softened

1 egg, separated

¼ cup (55g) caster (superfine) sugar

1 teaspoon vanilla extract

1½ cups (185g) plain (all-purpose) flour

3 medium mangoes (1.3kg)

60g (2 ounces) butter, extra

¼ cup (55g) raw sugar

2 tablespoons water

2 tablespoons demerara sugar

1 Preheat oven to 200°C/400°F.
2 Beat butter, egg yolk, caster sugar and extract in a small bowl with an electric mixer until light and fluffy. Transfer to a medium bowl; stir in sifted flour. Knead dough on floured surface until smooth, enclose in plastic wrap; refrigerate for 30 minutes.
3 Remove cheeks from mangoes; using a large metal spoon, scoop flesh from skin. Cut each cheek into three wedges. Melt extra butter in an ovenproof frying pan (base measurement 20cm (8-inch) and 5cm (2-inch) deep). Add raw sugar and the water; stir over heat, without boiling, until sugar dissolves. Simmer, uncovered, without stirring, for about 3 minutes or until light caramel in colour and thickened slightly. Place mango wedges in pan; cook for 2 minutes. Remove pan from heat; cool.
4 Roll out pastry between sheets of baking paper until large enough to generously cover mango in pan. Lift pastry over mango, tucking edges around fruit. Brush pastry lightly with egg white; sprinkle with demerara sugar.
5 Bake tart for about 30 minutes or until pastry is browned lightly. Stand in the pan for 5 minutes before carefully inverting tart onto serving plate.

TIP **Tart must be served on the same day it's made.**

PANETTONE TIRAMISU

PREP TIME 30 MINUTES **SERVES** 12

1kg (2-pound) panettone (see Tips)

½ cup (125ml) just-made strong coffee

2 tablespoons caster (superfine) sugar

½ cup (125ml) marsala

3 x 250g (8-ounce) packaged mascarpone

2 cups (500ml) ready-made thick vanilla dairy custard

50g (1½ ounces) dark (semi-sweet) chocolate

50g (1½ ounces) vienna almonds, chopped coarsely

6 medium fresh figs (360g), torn in half

2 tablespoons honey

1   Using a sharp knife, score a line around panettone at equal intervals into four layers. Holding a serrated knife horizontally, using score marks as a guide, cut panettone into four layers, starting at top.
2   Stir coffee, sugar and marsala in a small jug until sugar dissolves; cool.
3   Beat ¼ cup marsala mixture with mascarpone and custard in a large bowl with an electric mixer until almost firm peaks form.
4   Place base layer of panettone onto a large serving plate; brush with a little remaining marsala mixture. Spread with one-fifth mascarpone mixture; grate enough chocolate over to lightly coat. Repeat to make another three layers, finishing with mascarpone mixture. (For top panettone layer, brush underside with coffee syrup.) Top mascarpone mixture with vienna almonds and figs. Drizzle figs with honey to serve.

TIPS To assist with slicing the panettone, place it in the freezer for 1 hour to firm, alternatively refrigerate it overnight.
The panettone tiramisu can be made the night before, if preferred.

THE-NIGHT-BEFORE CHRISTMAS FROZEN ICE-CREAM CAKE

PREP TIME 20 MINUTES (+ FREEZING) **SERVES** 8

800g (1½–pound) square dark fruit cake

550g (1 pound) frozen mixed berries

1 litre (4 cups) good-quality vanilla bean ice-cream

2 tablespoons brandy or rum

½ teaspoon ground nutmeg

1½ teaspoons finely grated mandarin or orange rind

¼ cup (40g) dry-roasted almonds, chopped coarsely

10 vanilla-flavoured mini meringue drops

1 Grease a 20cm (8-inch) round springform pan; line base and side with baking paper, extending paper 3cm (1½ inches) above rim.
2 Cut fruit cake into three slices horizontally. Place a square slice in the centre of the base of the pan. Using remaining slices, trim them to fit the gaps; reserve trimmings. Using your hands, flatten fruit cake to form a level base without gaps. Cut trimmings into small pieces.
3 Remove ½ cup frozen red berries, cut any strawberries in half. Press strawberries to the side of the pan using some ice-cream as 'glue'. Place the pan in the freezer for 10 minutes.
4 Spoon remaining ice-cream into a large bowl; stir in brandy, nutmeg, rind and almonds. Spoon one-third of the ice-cream mixture into the pan; scatter with one-third reserved fruit cake, level with a spoon. Repeat with remaining ice-cream mixture and fruit cake. Freeze for 4 hours or overnight until firm.
5 To serve, transfer cake to a serving plate. Layer remaining berries and meringues over the top, crushing some of the meringues in the process.

TIP The cake can be made up to three days ahead.

CHOCOLATE CARAMEL SEMIFREDDO

PREP TIME 30 MINUTES (+ FREEZING) **SERVES** 10

You will need to start the recipe the day before.

2 x 360g (11½-ounce) packets plain or chocolate chip Belgian waffles (see Tips)

2 x 380g (12-ounce) cans caramel top 'n' fill

500g (1 pound) cream cheese, chopped, softened

2 tablespoons amaretto liqueur (optional)

2 x 50g (1½-ounce) chocolate-coated honeycomb bars, chopped coarsely

3 medium oranges (720g), peeled, sliced thinly

2 mandarins, peeled, segmented (see Tips)

1 cup (250ml) bottled salted caramel sauce

1 Grease a 24cm (9½-inch) round springform pan; line base and side with baking paper, extending paper 3cm (1¼ inches) beyond rim.

2 Trim waffles straight lengthways, following the natural waffle pattern. Place approximately five waffles, lengthways around inside edge of pan to create a collar. Trim remaining waffles horizontally on both sides to flatten and remove waffle pattern; place in base of pan, trimming to fit.

3 Beat caramel, cream cheese and liqueur in a large bowl with an electric mixer until smooth and well combined. Fold in half the honeycomb bar. Spoon mixture into the waffle-lined pan; smooth level. Freeze overnight.

4 To serve, top cake with orange slices, mandarin segments and remaining honeycomb bar. Drizzle with a little caramel sauce. Serve frozen slices, drizzled with remaining sauce.

TIPS If fresh mandarins are unavailable, you can use 310g (10 ounces) canned mandarin segments.

Amaretto is an almond-flavoured liqueur. You could also use an orange, coffee or hazelnut-flavoured liqueur instead.

TROPICAL SPLICE WITH MOJITO FRUIT SALAD

PREP + COOK TIME 1 HOUR (+ FREEZING & REFRIGERATION) **SERVES** 8

You will need to start this recipe the day before.

1 litre (4 cups) mango sorbet (see Tips)

1 litre (4 cups) good-quality vanilla bean ice-cream

2 teaspoons finely grated lime rind

½ cup (110g) caster (superfine) sugar

¾ cup (180ml) water

1 lime, cut into eight wedges, wedges halved

¼ cup (60ml) strained lime juice

½ cup (125ml) white rum

1 medium pineapple (1.25kg), peeled, quartered, cored, sliced thinly

1 medium mango (430g), sliced thinly

1 medium kiwifruit (85g), cut into thin wedges

⅓ cup (80ml) passionfruit pulp

½ cup baby or micro mint sprigs

1   Grease an 11cm x 25cm (4½-inch x 10-inch), 1.5-litre (6-cup) loaf pan; line base and long sides with baking paper, extending paper 5cm (2 inches) above edge. Lightly grease paper. Repeat, lining base and short sides. Spoon sorbet into pan; smooth surface. Cover; freeze for 1 hour or until firm.

2   Scoop ice-cream over sorbet layer, scattering with lime rind as you go; smooth surface. Cover; freeze for 2 hours or overnight until firm.

3   Reserve 1 tablespoon of the sugar. Stir remaining sugar and the water in a medium saucepan over medium heat, without boiling, until sugar dissolves. Bring to the boil; boil, uncovered, for 1 minute.

4   Place lime wedges and remaining sugar in a large heatproof bowl, using the end of a rolling pin, crush lime wedges. Pour over warm sugar syrup, lime juice, rum. Add pineapple, mango, kiwifruit and passionfruit; toss gently to combine. Refrigerate until required.

5   Rub the outside of the loaf pan with a warm, damp cloth. Invert pan onto serving platter, remove lining paper; cut into thick slices. Serve with fruit salad and mint sprigs.

TIPS You can also top the splice with toasted coconut flakes and extra lime rind, if you like.

PAVLOVA BAR

PREP TIME 15 MINUTES **SERVES** 6

300ml thickened (heavy) cream

1½ tablespoons icing (confectioners') sugar

237ml bottle ginger syrup

2 kaffir lime leaves, crushed

6 small peaches or nectarines (600g), halved, stones removed

1 small papaya (650g), halved, seeds removed, cut into thin wedges

3 passionfruit, halved

6 bought meringues or meringue nests

edible flowers (optional), to serve

1   Just before serving, beat cream and sifted icing sugar in a medium bowl with an electric mixer until soft peaks form. Transfer to a serving bowl.

2   Place ginger syrup in a small jug with crushed kaffir lime leaves.

3   Place peaches in a bowl; pour over 2 tablespoons of the ginger syrup. Arrange remaining fruit in separate bowls and place meringues on a cake stand, scattered with flowers, for guests to assemble pavlovas themselves.

TIPS You can try other fruit combinations: Berries & melon – serve bowls of raspberries, blueberries, strawberries and mulberries with melon ball scoops of watermelon splashed with rosewater. Golden fruit – serve bowls of passionfruit, yellow kiwifruit, pineapple and mango with toasted macadamias.

GOLDEN BOILED PUDDING

PREP + COOK TIME 3 HOURS 40 MINUTES (+ STANDING) **SERVES** 16

You will need to start this recipe a day ahead.

1 cup (180g) finely chopped dried pears

1 cup (130g) finely chopped dried cranberries

1 cup (75g) finely chopped dried apples

½ cup (80g) finely chopped dried apricots

1 large apple (200g), peeled, grated

⅓ cup (80ml) orange-flavoured liqueur

2 teaspoons finely grated orange rind

2 tablespoons orange juice

250g (8 ounces) butter, softened

1½ cups (330g) caster (superfine) sugar

4 eggs

1 cup (150g) plain (all-purpose) flour

½ teaspoon bicarbonate of soda (baking soda)

1 teaspoon ground cinnamon

3 cups (210g) stale breadcrumbs

1 cup (120g) ground almonds

⅔ cup (100g) plain (all-purpose) flour, extra

1 Combine fruit, liqueur, rind and juice in a large bowl. Cover; stand at room temperature overnight.

2 Beat butter and sugar in a small bowl with an electric mixer until combined; beat in eggs, one at a time. Stir butter mixture into fruit mixture; stir in sifted flour, soda and cinnamon, then breadcrumbs and ground almonds.

3 Fill a boiler three-quarters full of hot water, cover with a tight lid; bring to the boil. Have ready 1-metre (1-yard) length of kitchen string and extra plain flour. Wearing thick rubber gloves, dip pudding cloth into the boiling water. Boil for 1 minute then remove; squeeze excess water from cloth. Quickly spread hot cloth on bench. Rub flour into the centre of cloth to cover an area about 40cm (16 inches) in diameter, leaving flour a little thicker in centre of cloth where "skin" on pudding needs to be thickest.

4 Place pudding mixture in centre of cloth. Gather cloth evenly around mixture, avoiding any deep pleats; pat into a round shape. Tie cloth tightly with string as close to mixture as possible. Pull ends of cloth tightly to ensure pudding is as round and as firm as possible; tie loops in string.

5 Lower pudding into the boiling water; tie ends of string to handles of boiler to suspend pudding. Cover with tight lid; boil for 3 hours, replenishing with boiling water as necessary to maintain water level.

6 Untie pudding from handles; place a wooden spoon through string loops. Do not put pudding on bench; suspend from the spoon by placing over rungs of an upturned stool or wedging handle in a drawer. Twist ends of cloth around string to avoid them touching pudding; hang pudding for 10 minutes.

7 Place pudding on board; cut string, carefully peel back cloth. Turn pudding onto a plate then carefully peel cloth away completely. Stand at least 20 minutes or until skin darkens and pudding becomes firm. Serve dusted with sifted icing (confectioners') sugar, if you like.

TIPS You need an 80cm (32-inch) square of unbleached calico for the pudding cloth. If calico has not been used before, soak it in cold water overnight; the next day, boil it for 20 minutes then rinse in cold water. We used Grand Marnier in this recipe, but you can use your favourite orange-flavoured liqueur.

This recipe will make two smaller puddings; use two 40cm (16-inch) squares of calico to make the smaller puddings. Boil puddings in separate boilers for 2 hours. If you only have one boiler, the pudding mixture will stand at room temperature while you cook the first one.

GIFTS

GINGERBREAD GIFT TAGS

PREP + COOK TIME 1 HOUR (+ REFRIGERATION) **MAKES** 30 (10 OF EACH)

125g (4 ounces) butter, softened

½ cup (110g) firmly packed brown sugar

1 egg yolk

2½ cups (375g) plain (all-purpose) flour

1 teaspoon bicarbonate of soda
(baking soda)

3 teaspoons ground ginger

½ cup (125ml) golden syrup or treacle

ribbon

ROYAL ICING

1 egg white

1½ cups (240g) pure icing sugar (pure
confectioners' sugar), approximately

1   Preheat oven to 180°C/350°F. Grease three oven trays.

2   Beat butter and sugar in a small bowl with an electric mixer until combined. Beat in egg yolk. Stir in sifted dry ingredients and golden syrup to a soft dough. Knead dough on a floured surface until smooth. Divide dough into 2 portions. Roll each portion between sheets of baking paper until 3mm (⅛-inch) thick. Refrigerate for 1 hour.

3   Using an 8cm (3¼-inch) gingerbread-man cutter, cut out 10 shapes from one sheet of dough, re-rolling as necessary; place on tray about 3cm (1¼ inches) apart. Using a 7cm (2¾-inch) and a 10cm (4-inch) snowflake cutter, cut 10 of each snowflake from remaining sheet of dough, re-rolling as necessary; place on trays, about 3cm (1¼ inches) apart. Refrigerate all gingerbread for 30 minutes.

4   Using a large plastic straw cut two holes in each gingerbread shape, using picture as a guide. Bake gingerbread for 12 minutes and stars for 10 minutes or until lightly browned. (You may need to re-cut holes while the gingerbread is still warm.) Cool on trays.

5   Meanwhile, make royal icing.

6   Spoon icing into a piping bag fitted with a small plain tube; decorate shapes as desired. Stand at room temperature until set. Thread ribbon through holes.

ROYAL ICING

Beat egg white in a small bowl with electric mixer until frothy; gradually beat in enough sifted icing sugar to give a mixture of piping consistency. Keep royal icing covered with a damp tea towel to prevent it drying out.

STORAGE Gingerbread will keep, at room temperature, in an airtight container, for up to 1 week.

MINI FRUIT MINCE CAKES

PREP + COOK TIME 40 MINUTES (+ COOLING) **MAKES** 40

Enjoy a little bite of Christmas when you eat these mini cupcakes. Using store-bought mince, these cupcakes are quick and simple to make but full of festive cheer.

1⅓ cups (200g) self-raising flour

⅓ cup (75g) firmly packed light brown sugar

1½ cups (440g) fruit mince

½ cup (125ml) olive oil

⅓ cup (80ml) milk

1 egg

250g (8 ounces) white ready-made icing

¼ cup (40g) pure icing sugar (pure confectioners' sugar)

cachous

1   Preheat oven to 200°C/400°F. Line 40 holes of four 12-hole (1-tablespoon/20ml) mini muffin pans with paper cases.

2   Sift flour and brown sugar into a large bowl.

3   Whisk fruit mince, oil, milk and egg in a medium bowl until combined; stir into flour mixture until barely combined.

4   Drop level tablespoons of mixture into paper cases; bake about 15 minutes. Cool cakes in pans.

5   Knead icing on a surface dusted with sifted icing sugar until smooth. Roll out icing until 3mm (⅛-inch) thick; cut out small stars. Brush a tiny amount of water onto backs of stars; position on cakes. Press cachous into centres of stars before icing dries.

TIP We used 1.5cm (¾-inch), 2.5cm (1-inch) and 3cm (1¼-inch) cutters to make the stars.

STORAGE Cakes will keep in an airtight container at room temperature for up to 1 week.

NUTTY CHOC-CHIP BOILED FRUIT CAKES

PREP + COOK TIME 2 HOURS (+ COOLING & STANDING) **MAKES** 6

185g (6 ounces) butter, chopped

2¼ cups (375g) sultanas

1½ cups (250g) coarsely chopped raisins

½ cup (140g) peanut butter

1 cup (220g) firmly packed dark brown sugar

1 cup (250ml) hazelnut or chocolate-flavoured liqueur

180g (5½ ounces) dark (semi-sweet) chocolate, chopped coarsely

½ cup (70g) roasted unsalted peanuts, chopped coarsely

¾ cup (120g) almond kernels, chopped coarsely

½ cup (50g) roasted walnuts, chopped coarsely

¾ cup (110g) roasted unsalted macadamias, chopped coarsely

4 eggs

1¾ cups (360g) plain (all-purpose) flour

¼ cup (35g) self-raising flour

½ cup (70g) roasted unsalted peanuts, extra, chopped coarsely

½ cup (80g) almond kernels, extra, chopped coarsely

½ cup (50g) roasted walnuts, extra, chopped coarsely

½ cup (70g) roasted unsalted macadamias, extra, chopped coarsely

TOFFEE

1½ cups (330g) caster (superfine) sugar

½ cup (125ml) water

1 Place butter in a large saucepan with fruit, peanut butter, sugar and liqueur; stir over medium heat, without boiling, until sugar dissolves. Bring to the boil. Reduce heat; simmer, covered, for 10 minutes. Transfer mixture to a large bowl; cool.

2 Preheat oven to 130°C/260°F. Grease six deep 10cm (4-inch) square cake pans; line base and sides with two thicknesses of baking paper, extending paper 5cm (2 inches) above sides.

3 Stir chocolate and nuts into fruit mixture with lightly beaten eggs and sifted flours. Spread mixture evenly into pans.

4 Bake cakes about 1 hour. Cover hot cakes with foil; turn cakes upside-down. Cool cakes in pans overnight.

5 Make toffee.

6 Coarsely chop extra nuts. Drizzle one of the cakes with a little toffee; press some of the nuts on top. Drizzle with a little more toffee to glaze. Repeat with remaining cakes, toffee and nuts. Stand until set.

TOFFEE

Stir sugar and the water in a small saucepan over high heat, without boiling, until sugar dissolves. Bring to the boil; boil, uncovered, without stirring, about 10 minutes or until caramel in colour.

TIPS Use frangelico (hazelnut) or crème de cacao (chocolate) flavoured liqueurs. Cut cakes with a serrated knife.

STORAGE Cakes will keep in an airtight container at room temperature for up to 4 weeks; the toffee will soften after a few days.

WHITE CHOC-MINT CANDY CANE BARK

PREP + COOK TIME 10 MINUTES (+ REFRIGERATION) **SERVES** 16

375g (12 ounces) white chocolate melts

1¼ cups (45g) rice bubbles

⅓ cup (25g) shredded coconut

75g (2½ ounces) candy canes, chopped coarsely

1 tablespoon silver cachous

1 tablespoon tiny silver cachous

1   Grease a 23cm x 32cm (9-inch x 13-inch) swiss roll pan. Line with baking paper.
2   Place chocolate into a medium heatproof bowl; stir over a medium saucepan of simmering water until smooth (don't let water touch base of bowl). Stir in rice bubbles and coconut. Working quickly, spread chocolate mixture onto tray as thinly as possible; sprinkle with candy canes and cachous. Refrigerate until set.
3   Break bark into pieces to serve.

   TIP We used two different sizes of silver cachous but you can use whatever you have available.

SUPER SEED BRITTLE

PREP + COOK TIME 35 MINUTES (+ STANDING) **SERVES** 16

2 cups (440g) caster (superfine) sugar

½ cup (125ml) water

½ cup (100g) pepitas (pumpkin seeds), toasted

½ cup (75g) sunflower seeds, toasted

1 tablespoon sesame seeds, toasted

1 tablespoon black chia seeds

1 Line an oven tray with baking paper.

2 Combine sugar and the water in a medium saucepan; stir over medium heat, without boiling, until sugar dissolves. Bring to the boil; boil, uncovered, without stirring, until golden brown. Allow bubbles to subside; add seeds. Pour mixture onto tray; leave to set at room temperature.

3 Break brittle into pieces to serve.

TIP Chia seeds come from a plant that is related to mint. They are a source of fibre and omega-3 fats.

RUM, RAISIN AND CRANBERRY CHOCOLATE CAKES

PREP + COOK TIME 45 MINUTES (+ COOLING) **MAKES** 18

185g (6 ounces) unsalted butter, chopped

300g (9½ ounces) dark (semi-sweet) chocolate, chopped coarsely

¼ cup (25g) cocoa powder

1 cup (220g) firmly packed light brown sugar

¾ cup (165g) caster (superfine) sugar

2 teaspoons vanilla extract

4 eggs

1½ cups (225g) plain (all-purpose) flour

¼ cup (60ml) dark rum

½ cup (75g) raisins, chopped coarsely

½ cup (65g) dried cranberries, chopped coarsely

½ cup (70g) roasted unsalted shelled pistachios, chopped coarsely

1 Preheat oven to 170°C/340°F. Line 18 holes of two 12-hole (⅓-cup/80ml) muffin pans with paper cases.
2 Place butter and chocolate in a large saucepan; stir over low heat until smooth. Whisk in sifted cocoa and sugars; cool 15 minutes.
3 Stir in extract and lightly beaten eggs, then sifted flour and rum. Stir raisins, half the cranberries and half the nuts into chocolate mixture. Spoon mixture evenly into paper cases; sprinkle with remaining cranberries and nuts.
4 Bake about 30 minutes. Cool cakes in pan.

TIP These fudgy cakes are delicious served warm or cold. For a delicious dessert, remove cakes from paper cases and place on a serving plate; reheat each cake in microwave and serve with double cream or vanilla ice-cream.

CHOCOLATE BONBONS

PREP + COOK TIME 20 MINUTES (+ REFRIGERATION) **MAKES** 24

125g (4 ounces) turkish delight

⅓ cup (45g) roasted unsalted shelled pistachios, chopped coarsely

40g (1½ ounces) mini white marshmallows

⅓ cup (45g) dried cranberries

370g (12 ounces) dark (semi-sweet) chocolate, chopped coarsely

1   Using lightly oiled scissors, chop turkish delight into small squares.
2   Sprinkle half of the turkish delight, nuts, marshmallows and cranberries into holes of two 12-hole (1-tablespoon/20ml) silicone mini muffin pans.
3   Stir chocolate in a medium saucepan, over low heat, until smooth. Pour chocolate into pan holes, making sure chocolate runs to the base. Sprinkle tops with remaining turkish delight, nuts, marshmallows and cranberries; press gently into chocolate. Refrigerate about 2 hours or until set.
4   Turn bonbons out of pans; wrap individually in cellophane.

TIP If you don't have a silicone pan, turn this recipe into a rustic 'rocky road'. Melt the chocolate and mix with the remaining ingredients; spread into a shallow baking-paper-lined tray and, when it's almost set, cut into squares.

STORAGE Store bonbons in an airtight container in the fridge.

CHOCOLATE PISTACHIO SHORTBREAD

PREP + COOK TIME 1¼ HOURS (+ COOLING) **MAKES** 6 ROUNDS

The ultimate Christmas indulgence – these cookies are full of rich and luxurious ingredients – cocoa, butter, sugar and pistachios – it will be hard to stop them disappearing from the cookie jar.

½ cup (70g) roasted unsalted shelled pistachios

250g (8 ounces) unsalted butter, softened

1 cup (160g) icing (confectioners') sugar

1¼ cups (185g) plain (all-purpose) flour

½ cup (100g) rice flour

⅓ cup (35g) dutch cocoa powder

1 Preheat oven to 160°C/325°F. Line two large oven trays with baking paper.
2 Process half the nuts until finely ground; finely chop remaining nuts.
3 Beat butter and sifted icing sugar in a small bowl with an electric mixer until light and fluffy. Transfer mixture to a large bowl; stir in sifted flours, cocoa and ground nuts, in two batches. Turn dough onto a floured surface; knead until smooth.
4 Divide dough into six portions, place three portions on each tray. Using hands, press each portion into a 12cm (4¾-inch) round, so the rounds are about 2.5cm (1-inch) apart. Using fingers, pinch edges of rounds to make frills. Mark each round into 6 wedges; prick wedges with a fork. Sprinkle rounds with chopped nuts.
5 Bake about 45 minutes. Cool shortbreads on trays before cutting into wedges.

STORAGE Shortbreads will keep in an airtight container at room temperature for up to 2 weeks.

4 *Ways with* EDIBLE GIFTS

LATTE SHORTBREAD STARS

PREP + COOK TIME 40 MINUTES **MAKES** ABOUT 55

Preheat oven to 160°C/325°F. Line oven trays with baking paper. Beat 250g (8oz) softened butter, ¼ cup caster (superfine) sugar and 1 teaspoon vanilla extract in a small bowl with an electric mixer until smooth. Transfer to a large bowl; stir in 1½ cups sifted plain (all-purpose) flour, in two batches. Dissolve 4 teaspoons instant coffee granules in 1 teaspoon boiling water; stir coffee mixture into dough. Refrigerate until firm. Roll dough between sheets of baking paper until 5mm (¼ inch) thick. Using assorted star-shaped cutters, cut shapes from dough; place on trays. Bake about 15 minutes. Sprinkle with ¼ cup demerara sugar; cool on trays.

CHOC-ORANGE MERINGUES

PREP + COOK TIME 1 HOUR 25 MINUTES (+ COOLING & STANDING) **MAKES** 25

Preheat oven to 120°C/250°F. Grease oven trays; line with baking paper. Beat 3 egg whites in a small bowl with an electric mixer until soft peaks form. Gradually add ¾ cup caster (superfine) sugar, beating until dissolved between additions. Fold 1 tablespoon sifted cocoa powder and 2 teaspoons finely grated orange rind into meringue mixture until just combined. Drop level tablespoons of mixture onto trays 2cm (¾ inch) apart. Bake about 1 hour. Cool on trays. Drizzle meringues with 90g (3oz) melted dark (semi-sweet) chocolate; stand at room temperature until set.

HONEY AND COCONUT MUESLI BARS

PREP + COOK TIME 50 MINUTES **MAKES** 36

Preheat oven to 160°C/325°F. Grease a 23cm x 32cm (9-in x 13-in) swiss roll pan; line base and long sides with baking paper, extending the paper 5cm (2in) over sides. Combine 2½ cups rolled oats, 1 cup rice bubbles, ½ cup shredded coconut, ½ cup slivered almonds, 1 tablespoon honey and 395g (14oz) canned sweetened condensed milk in a large bowl. Press mixture firmly into pan. Bake for 40 minutes or until browned lightly. Cool in pan.

CHOCOLATE BROWNIE SLICE

PREP + COOK TIME 1 HOUR **MAKES** 25

Preheat oven to 180°C/350°F. Grease a deep 20cm (8-in) square cake pan; line base and sides with baking paper, extending the paper 5cm (2 inches) over sides. Stir 200g (6½oz) chopped butter and 200g (6½oz) chopped dark (semi-sweet) chocolate in a medium saucepan over low heat until smooth. Cool for 10 minutes. Stir in ¾ cup caster (superfine) sugar and 2 eggs, then 1 cup sifted plain (all-purpose) flour, 155g (5oz) chopped white chocolate and 90g (3oz) chopped milk chocolate. Spread mixture into pan. Bake about 35 minutes. Cool in pan.

CINNAMON EGGNOGG MACARONS

PREP + COOK TIME 45 MINUTES (+ STANDING & COOLING) **MAKES** 16

1¼ cups (200g) icing (confectioners') sugar

¾ cup (90g) ground almonds

¼ cup (20g) desiccated coconut

1 teaspoon ground cinnamon

3 egg whites

¼ cup (55g) caster (superfine) sugar

2 teaspoons icing (confectioners') sugar, extra

EGGNOG CUSTARD

1 tablespoon cornflour (cornstarch)

1 tablespoon custard powder

1 tablespoon caster (superfine) sugar

½ cup (125ml) milk

15g (½ ounce) butter

1 egg yolk

2 tablespoons brandy

1 Grease and line oven trays.

2 Process icing sugar, ground almonds, coconut and cinnamon until fine; sift through a fine sieve into a medium bowl, discard any large pieces.

3 Beat egg whites and caster sugar in a small bowl with an electric mixer until firm peaks form and sugar is dissolved. Fold in almond mixture, in two batches.

4 Spoon mixture into a piping bag fitted with a 1cm (½-inch) plain tube. Pipe 4cm (1½-inch) rounds, about 2.5cm (1-inch) apart, on trays. Tap trays on bench so macarons spread slightly. Dust with sifted extra icing sugar. Stand about 30 minutes or until macarons are dry to touch.

5 Make eggnog custard.

6 Preheat oven to 150°C/300°F.

7 Bake macarons about 20 minutes. Cool on trays.

8 Sandwich macarons with about 1 teaspoon of custard.

EGGNOG CUSTARD

Combine cornflour, custard powder and sugar in a small saucepan; gradually stir in milk. Stir over heat until mixture boils and thickens. Remove from heat; stir in butter, egg yolk and brandy. Cover surface with plastic wrap; cool.

TIP The custard can be made several days ahead; store in the fridge. Return custard to room temperature before using.

STORAGE Filled macarons are best eaten the day they are made. Unfilled macarons will keep in an airtight container, at room temperature, for up to 3 days or will freeze for 3 months.

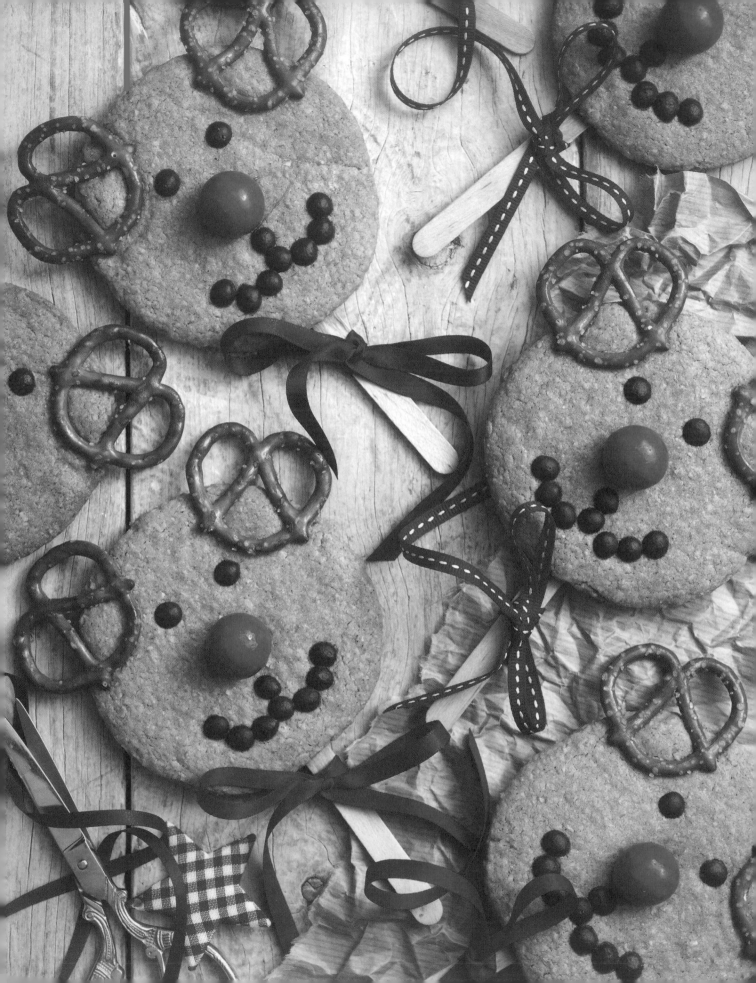

RUDOLF THE REINDEER COOKIES

PREP + COOK TIME 45 MINUTES (+ REFRIGERATION & COOLING) **MAKES** 10

90g (3 ounces) butter, softened

1 egg

⅓ cup (110g) firmly packed light brown sugar

⅓ cup (25g) desiccated coconut

⅓ cup (35g) wheat germ

⅔ cup (100g) wholemeal plain (all-purpose) flour

⅓ cup (50g) white self-raising flour

½ teaspoon mixed spice

20 pretzels (40g)

¼ cup (45g) dark choc Bits

10 giant choc orange balls (70g)

1 Beat butter, egg and sugar in a small bowl with an electric mixer until combined. Stir in coconut, wheat germ, sifted flours and spice. Wrap dough in plastic wrap; refrigerate for 30 minutes.

2 Roll dough between sheets of baking paper until 5mm (¼-inch) thick. Place on a tray; refrigerate 30 minutes.

3 Preheat oven to 180°C/350°F. Grease and line oven trays with baking paper.

4 Using a 9cm (3¼-inch) round cutter, cut 10 rounds from dough, re-rolling scraps as necessary. Place rounds about 7.5cm (3-inches) apart on trays. Slide an ice-block stick under each cookie; press down firmly. Position two pretzels on each cookie for antlers; press down firmly. Decorate cookies with choc Bits for eyes and mouths. Bake about 12 minutes.

5 Immediately press choc orange balls onto hot cookies for noses. Cool on trays.

> TIPS **You need 10 ice-block sticks. If the choc orange balls don't stick to the cookies, secure them with a little melted chocolate.**
>
> STORAGE **completed cookies can be stored in an airtight container for up to 1 week.**

4 *Special* GIFT IDEAS

SWEET CHILLI SAUCE

PREP + COOK TIME 1 HOUR 15 MINUTES **MAKES** 3 CUPS

Remove green stems from 250g (8oz) fresh long red chillies; chop chillies coarsely with their seeds. Process chilli until finely chopped. Combine 3 cups white vinegar, 2 cups water, 2 cups white (granulated) sugar and 2 teaspoons salt in a large saucepan; stir over low heat, without boiling, until sugar dissolves. Add chilli; boil, uncovered, for 20 minutes. Add 6 crushed cloves garlic; boil, uncovered, for about 20 minutes or until mixture is reduced to 3 cups. The sauce will thicken on cooling. Stand sauce for 10 minutes. Pour hot sauce into hot sterilised bottles; seal immediately. Cool; refrigerate.

STORAGE Sauce will keep, refrigerated, for up to two months.

JEWELLED ROCKY ROAD

PREP + COOK TIME 20 MINUTES (+ REFRIGERATION) **MAKES** 35

Grease a 20cm x 30cm (8-inch x 12-inch) rectangular slice pan; line base and long sides with baking paper, extending paper 5cm (2 inches) over sides. Combine 300g (9½oz) coarsely chopped toasted marshmallows with coconut, ½ cup roasted flaked almonds, 4 coarsely chopped slices glacé pineapple (125g), ½ cup coarsely chopped glacé peaches and ½ cup (100g) coarsely chopped glacé citron in a large bowl. Working quickly, stir in 450g (14½oz) melted white chocolate; spread mixture into pan, push mixture down firmly to flatten. Refrigerate rocky road until set before cutting into squares.

TIP You can use ½ cup coarsely chopped green glacé cherries instead of the glacé citron.

IRISH CRÈME LIQUEUR

PREP TIME 10 MINUTES (+ REFRIGERATION)
MAKES 1.25 LITRES (5 CUPS)

Dissolve 1 tablespoon instant coffee granules in
1 tablespoon boiling water in a large jug; stir in
1½ tablespoons chocolate-flavoured topping.
Whisk in 350ml Irish whiskey, 1¾ cups pouring
cream, 395g (12½oz) canned sweetened condensed
milk, 1 egg, 1 teaspoon coconut essence. Strain
mixture into cooled sterilised bottles; seal immediately.

TIP Store liqueur in refrigerator for up to 6 months.

ALMOND BREAD

PREP + COOK TIME 1 HOUR 35 MINUTES
(+ COOLING & STANDING) **MAKES** 40 SLICES

Preheat oven to 180°C/350°F. Grease a 10cm x 20cm
(4-inch x 8-inch) loaf pan. Beat 3 egg whites in a small bowl
with an electric mixer until soft peaks form. Gradually add
½ cup caster (superfine) sugar, beating until dissolved
between additions. Fold 1 cup plain (all-purpose) sifted
flour and ¾ cup almond kernels into egg white mixture;
spread mixture into pan. Bake about 30 minutes. Cool
bread in pan. Remove bread from pan, wrap in foil; stand
overnight. Preheat oven to 150°C/300°F. Using a sharp
serrated knife, cut the bread into wafer-thin slices. Place
slices, in a single layer, on ungreased oven trays. Bake
about 45 minutes or until dry and crisp.

GLOSSARY

ALLSPICE also called pimento or jamaican pepper; available whole or ground. Tastes like a blend of cinnamon, clove and nutmeg.

ALMONDS
blanched brown skins removed.
flaked paper-thin slices.
ground also known as almond meal.
slivered small pieces cut lengthways.
vienna toffee-coated almonds.

BALSAMIC VINEGAR
originally from Modena, Italy there are now many types on the market ranging in pungency and quality depending on how, and for how long they have been aged.

BAY LEAVES aromatic leaves from the bay tree available fresh or dried, adds a strong, slightly peppered taste. Remove from dish before stirring.

BEEF
eye-fillet tenderloin, fillet; fine texture, most expensive and extremely tender.
mince also known as ground beef.
rump boneless tender cut taken from the upper part of the round (hindquarter). Cut into steaks, good for barbecuing; as one piece, great as a roast.
sausages seasoned and spiced minced (ground) beef mixed with cereal and packed into casings.
scotch fillet cut from the muscle running behind the shoulder along the spine. Also known as cube roll, cuts include standing rib roast and rib-eye.
skirt steak lean, flavourful coarse-grained cut from the inner thigh. Needs slow-cooking; good for stews or casseroles.

BREADCRUMBS
fresh bread, usually white, processed into fine crumbs.
packaged prepared fine-textured but crunchy white breadcrumbs; good for coating foods that are to be fried.
panko (japanese) are available in two kinds: larger pieces and fine crumbs; have a lighter texture than Western-style ones. Available from Asian food stores and supermarkets.
stale crumbs made by grating, blending or processing 1- or 2-day old bread.

BROCCOLINI
a cross between broccoli and chinese kale; long asparagus-like stems with a long loose floret. Resembles broccoli but is milder and sweeter in taste.

BUK CHOY
also called bok choy, pak choi, chinese white cabbage or chinese chard; has a fresh, mild mustard taste.

BUTTER
we use salted butter unless stated otherwise; 125g is equal to 1 stick (4 ounces). Unsalted or "sweet" butter has no salt added and is perhaps the most popular butter among pastry-chefs.

CAPERS
the grey-green buds of a warm climate shrub, sold either dried and salted or pickled in a vinegar brine; tiny young ones, called baby capers, are available in brine or dried in salt.

CAPSICUM (BELL PEPPER)
comes in many colours: red, green, yellow, orange and purplish-black. Be sure to discard seeds and membranes before use.

CHEESE
cream commonly called philadelphia or philly; a soft cow-milk cheese; its fat content ranges from 14% to 33%.
fetta Greek in origin; a crumbly textured goat- or sheep-milk cheese having a sharp, salty taste. Ripened and stored in salted whey; particularly good tossed into salads.
goat's made from goat's milk, has an earthy, strong taste. Available in soft, crumbly and firm textures, in various shapes and sizes, and sometimes rolled in ash or herbs.
mascarpone an Italian fresh cultured-cream product made similarly to yogurt. Whiteish to creamy yellow in colour, with a buttery-rich, luscious texture, it is soft, creamy and spreadable.
mozzarella soft, spun-curd cheese; originating in southern Italy, it is the most popular pizza cheese because of its low melting point and elasticity when heated.
parmesan also called parmigiano; is a hard, grainy cow-milk cheese originating in Italy. Reggiano is the best variety.
pecorino the generic Italian name for cheeses made from sheep milk. This family of hard, white to pale-yellow cheeses, traditionally made in the Italian winter and spring when sheep graze on natural pastures, has been matured for 8 to 12 months. If you can't find it, use parmesan cheese.
ricotta a soft, sweet, moist, white cow-milk cheese with a low-fat content and a slightly grainy texture. The name roughly translates as "cooked again" and refers to ricotta's manufacture from a whey that is a by-product of other cheese making.

CHICKEN
breast fillet breast halved, skinned and boned.
thigh skin and bone intact.
thigh fillets skin and bone removed.

CHICKPEAS (GARBANZO BEANS)
also called hummus or channa; an irregularly round, sandy-coloured legume. Firm texture even after cooking. Available canned or dried (reconstitute for several hours in cold water before use).

CHILLI
use rubber gloves when peparing fresh chillis as they can burn your skin. Removing membranes and seeds lessens the heat level.
flakes dried, deep-red, dehydrated chilli slices and seeds.
green any unripened chilli; also some particular varieties that are ripe when green, such as habanero or poblano.
long-red available both fresh and dried, a generic term for any moderately hot, thin, long (6-8cm/2¼-3¼ inch) chilli.
thai (serrano) also known as "scuds"; tiny, very hot and bright red in colour.

CHOCOLATE
dark (semi-sweet) also called luxury chocolate; made of a high percentage of cocoa liquor and cocoa butter, and a little added sugar. Dark chocolate is ideal for use in desserts and cakes.
milk most popular eating chocolate, mild and very sweet similar in make-up to dark with the difference being the addition of milk solids.
white contains no cocoa solids but derives its sweet flavour from cocoa butter. Very sensitive to heat.

CHORIZO SAUSAGES
a sausage of Spanish origin, made from coarsely minced (ground) smoked pork and highly seasoned with garlic, chilli powder and other spices.

CINNAMON
available in pieces (called sticks or quills) and ground into powder; one of the world's most common spices.

CLOVES
dried flower buds of a tropical tree; can be used whole or ground; has a strong scent and taste so use sparingly.

COCOA POWDER
also known as unsweetened cocoa; cocoa beans that have been fermented, roasted, shelled, ground into powder then cleared of most of the fat content.
dutch-processed is treated with an alkali to neutralise its acids. It has a reddish brown colour, a mild flavour and is easy to dissolve.

COCONUT
desiccated concentrated, dried, unsweetened and finely shredded coconut flesh.
flaked dried, flaked coconut flesh.
shredded unsweetened thin strips of dried coconut flesh.

CORIANDER (CILANTRO)
bright-green-leafed herb with a pungent aroma and taste. Dried coriander seeds are sold either whole or ground, and neither form tastes remotely like the fresh leaf.

CORNFLOUR (CORNSTARCH)
available made from corn (maize) or wheat; used as a thickening agent.

CRANBERRIES
available dried and frozen; have a rich, astringent flavour and can be used in cooking sweet and savoury dishes. The dried version can usually be substituted for or with other dried fruit.

CREAM
pouring also known as pure or fresh cream. It has no additives and contains a minimum fat content of 35%
thick (double) a dolloping cream with a minimum fat content of 45%.
thickened (heavy) a whipping cream that contains a thickener. It has a minimum fat content of 35%.

DUKKAH
an Egyptian specialty spice mixture made up of roasted nuts, seeds and an array of aromatic spices.

EGGPLANT
also called aubergine. Ranging in size from tiny to very large and in colour from pale green to deep purple. Can also be purchased char-grilled, packed in oil, in jars.

FENNEL
also called finocchio or anise; a crunchy green vegetable slightly resembling celery, eaten raw in salads; fried as an accompaniment; or used as an ingredient in soups and sauces. Also the name given to the dried seeds of the plant, which have a stronger licorice flavour.

FLOUR
plain (all-purpose) unbleached wheat flour, is the best for baking.
self-raising all-purpose plain flour sifted with added baking powder in the proportion of 1 cup flour to 2 teaspoons baking powder.

wholemeal also called wholewheat; milled with the wheat germ.

GOLDEN SYRUP
a by-product of refined sugarcane; pure maple syrup or honey can be substituted. Treacle is a similar product, however, it is more viscous and has a stronger flavour and aroma than golden syrup (which has been refined further and contains fewer impurities, so is lighter in colour and more fluid).

GINGER
fresh also called green or root ginger; the thick gnarled root of a tropical plant. Can be kept, peeled, covered with dry sherry in a jar and refrigerated, or frozen in an airtight container.
glacé fresh ginger root preserved in sugar syrup.
ground also called powdered ginger; used as a flavouring in baking but cannot be substituted for fresh ginger.

KAFFIR LIME LEAVES
also known as bai magrood and looks like two glossy dark-green leaves joined end to end, forming a rounded hourglass shape. Used fresh or dried in South-East Asian dishes, they are used like bay leaves or curry leaves. Sold fresh, dried or frozen, the dried leaves are less potent so double the number if using them as a substitute for fresh; a strip of fresh lime peel may be substituted for each kaffir lime leaf.

KUMARA (ORANGE SWEET POTATO)
Polynesian name of an orange-fleshed sweet potato often confused with yam; good baked, boiled, mashed or fried similarly to other potatoes.

LAMB
backstrap also known as eye of loin; the larger fillet from a row of loin chops or cutlets. Tender, best cooked rapidly: barbecued or pan-fried.
rolled shoulder boneless section of the forequarter, rolled and secured with string or netting.
shoulder large, tasty piece having much connective tissue so is best pot-roasted or braised. Makes the best mince.

LEMON GRASS
also known as takrai, serai or serah. A tall, clumping, lemon-smelling and tasting, sharp-edged aromatic tropical grass; the white lower part of the stem is used, finely chopped. Can be found, fresh, dried, powdered and frozen, in supermarkets, greengrocers and Asian food shops.

LENTILS
(red, brown, yellow) dried pulse often identified by and named after their colour. Lentils have a high food value.

MAPLE SYRUP
distilled from the sap of sugar maple trees. Most often eaten with pancakes or waffles, but also used as an ingredient in baking or in desserts. Maple-flavoured syrup or pancake syrup is not an adequate substitute for the real thing.

MARZIPAN
made from ground almonds, sugar and glucose. Similar to almond paste, however, is not as strong in flavour, has a finer consistency and is more pliable. Cheaper brands often use ground apricot kernels and sugar.

MIXED SPICE
a classic spice mixture generally containing caraway, allspice, coriander, cumin, nutmeg and ginger, although cinnamon and other spices can be added. It is used with fruit and in cakes.

MUSTARD
dijon also called french. Pale brown, creamy, distinctively flavoured, fairly mild french mustard.
wholegrain also known as seeded. A French-style coarse-grain mustard made from crushed mustard seeds and dijon-style french mustard. Works well with cold meats and sausages.

NUTMEG
a strong and pungent spice ground from the dried nut of an evergreen tree native to Indonesia. Usually found ground but the flavour is more intense from a whole nut, available from spice shops, so it's best to grate your own.

OIL
cooking spray we use a cholesterol-free spray made from canola oil.
olive made from ripened olives. Extra virgin and virgin are the first and second press, respectively, of the olives and are therefore considered the best; the "extra light" or "light" name on other types refers to taste not fat levels.
peanut pressed from ground peanuts; most commonly used oil in Asian cooking because of its high smoke point (capacity to handle high heat without burning).
sesame made from roasted, crushed, white sesame seeds; a flavouring rather than a cooking medium.

vegetable sourced from plant rather than animal fat.

ONIONS

brown and white are interchangeable; white onions are more pungent.

green (scallion) also called incorrectly shallot; an immature onion picked before the bulb has formed, has a long, bright green stalk.

red also known as spanish, red spanish or bermuda onion; a sweet-flavoured, large, purple-red onion.

shallots also called french shallots or eschalots; small and brown-skinned.

spring an onion with a small white bulb and long, narrow green-leafed tops.

PASTRY SHEETS ready-rolled packaged sheets of frozen puff and shortcrust pastry, available from supermarkets.

PEARL BARLEY a nutrious grain used in soups and stews; has had the husk removed then has been steamed and polished so only the "pearl" of the original grain remains.

PEPITAS (PUMPKIN SEEDS) are the pale green kernels of dried pumpkin seeds; they can be bought plain or salted.

POLENTA also called cornmeal; a ground, flour-like cereal made of dried corn (maize).

POMEGRANATE a fruit about the size of an orange, with a yellowish shell that turns a rich red colour as it matures. Inside the inedible husk are hundreds of seeds, each wrapped in an edible lucent-crimson pulp having a tangy sweet-sour flavour.

POMEGRANATE MOLASSES

not to be confused with pomegranate syrup or grenadine (used in cocktails); pomegranate molasses is thicker, browner, and more concentrated in flavour — tart and sharp, slightly sweet and fruity. Brush over grilling or roasting meat, seafood or poultry, add to salad dressings or sauces. Buy from Middle Eastern food stores or specialty food shops.

RHUBARB A plant with long, green-red stalks; becomes sweet and edible when cooked.

SAFFRON stigma of a member of the crocus family, available ground or in strands; imparts a yellow-orange colour to food once infused. The quality can vary greatly; the best is the most expensive spice in the world.

SUGAR

brown a very soft, finely granulated sugar that retains molasses for colour and flavour.

caster (superfine) finely granulated table sugar.

icing (confectioners') also known as powdered sugar; pulverised granulated sugar crushed together with a small amount of cornflour (cornstarch).

raw natural brown granulated sugar.

white (granulated) coarse, granulated table sugar, also called crystal sugar.

SUMAC a purple-red, astringent spice ground from berries growing on shrubs that flourish wild around the Mediterranean; adds a tart, lemony flavour to dips and dressings and goes well with barbecued meat. Can be found in Middle-Eastern food stores.

TOMATOES

bottled pasta sauce a prepared sauce; a blend of tomato, herbs and spices.

canned whole, peeled tomatoes in natural juices; available crushed, chopped or diced. Use undrained.

paste triple-concentrated tomato puree used to flavour soups, stews and sauces.

puree canned pureed tomatoes; not to be confused with tomato paste.

VANILLA

bean dried, long thin pod from a tropical golden orchid. the black seeds inside the bean impart a luscious flavour in baking and desserts.

extract obtained from vanilla beans infused in water.

paste made from vanilla beans. Is highly concentrated: 1 teaspoon replaces a whole vanilla bean.

YEAST dried and fresh, a raising agent used in dough making; granular (7g sachets) and fresh compressed (20g blocks) yeast can almost always be substituted for the other.

YOGHURT we use plain full-cream yoghurt in our recipes.

greek-style plain yoghurt strained in a cloth (traditionally muslin) to remove the whey and give it a creamy consistency.

ZUCCHINI also called courgette; small, pale- or dark-green or yellow vegetable.

INDEX

Published in 2016 by Bounty Books based on materials
licensed to it by Bauer Media Books, Australia.

Bauer Media Books is a division of Bauer Media Pty Limited,
54 Park St, Sydney; GPO Box 4088, Sydney, NSW 2001, Australia
phone (+61) 2 9282 8618; fax (+61) 2 9126 3702
www.awwcookbooks.com.au

BAUER MEDIA BOOKS
PUBLISHER Jo Runciman
EDITORIAL & FOOD DIRECTOR Pamela Clark
DIRECTOR OF SALES, MARKETING & RIGHTS Brian Cearnes
CREATIVE DIRECTOR Hannah Blackmore
SENIOR DESIGNER Meng Koach
DESIGNER Bernhard Schmitz
SENIOR EDITOR Kyle Rankin
FOOD EDITOR Rebecca Meli
OPERATIONS MANAGER David Scotto

Published and distributed in the United Kingdom by
Bounty Books, a division of Octopus Publishing Group Ltd
Carmelite House
50 Victoria Embankment
London, EC4Y 0DZ
United Kingdom
info@octopus-publishing.co.uk;
www.octopusbooks.co.uk

PRINTED BY Leo Paper Products Ltd, China.

INTERNATIONAL FOREIGN LANGUAGE RIGHTS
Brian Cearnes, Bauer Media Books
bcearnes@bauer-media.com.au

A catalogue record for this book is available
from the British Library.
ISBN: 9780753731260

© Bauer Media Pty Limited 2016
ABN 18 053 273 546

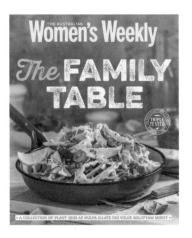